I0797298

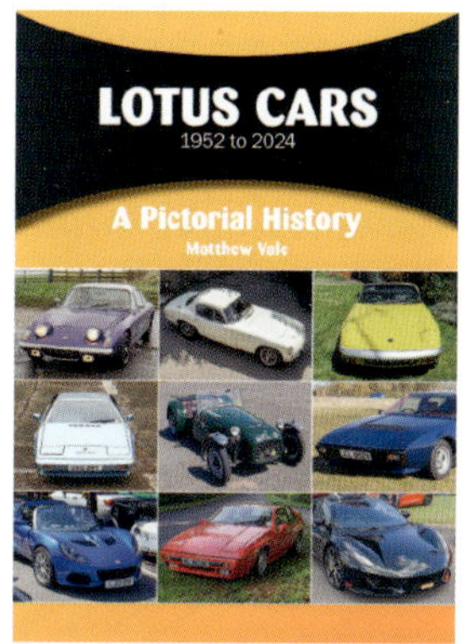
LOTUS CARS
1952 to 2024
A Pictorial History
Matthew Vale

A Pictorial History – more titles in this series

Austin Cars 1948 to 1990 (Rowe)
Bentley Cars (Taylor)
BMW Cars (Alder)
Citroën Cars 1934 to 1986 (Parish)
Ford Cars – Ford UK cars 1945-1995 (Rowe)
Jaguar Cars 1946 to 2008 (Thorley)
Mercedes Benz Cars 1947 to 2000 (Taylor)
MG Cars 1930 to 2006 (Alder)
Morris Cars 1948 to 1984 (Newell)
Riley & Wolseley Cars 1948 to 1975 (Rowe)
Rootes Cars of the 50s, 60s & 70s (Hillman, Humber, Singer, Sunbeam & Talbot) (Rowe)
Rover Cars 1945 to 2005 (Taylor)
Saab Cars 1949 to 2011 (Parish)
Triumph & Standard Cars 1945 to 1984 (Warrington)
Vauxhall Cars 1945 to 1995 (Alder)
Volvo Cars 1945 to 1995 (Alder)

More Lotus titles

Lotus Elan – S1 to Sprint and Plus 2 to Plus 2S 130/5 1962 to 1974 (Vale)
Lotus Elan and +2 Source Book (Vale)
Lotus Elite – Colin Chapman's first GT Car (Vale)
Lotus 49 - The Story of a Legend (Oliver)
Lotus Europa - Colin Chapman's mid-engined masterpiece (Vale)
Lotus Europa – S1, S2, Twin Cam & Special 1966 to 1975 (Vale)
Lotus Evora – Speed and Style (Tipler)
A Life in Car Design – Jaguar, Lotus, TVR (Winterbottom)

www.veloce.co.uk

First published in 2025 by Veloce, an imprint of David and Charles Limited. Tel +44 (0)1305 260068 / e-mail info@veloce.co.uk / web www.veloce.co.uk.

ISBN: 9781836440109 Readers with ideas for automotive books, or books on other transport or related hobby subjects, are invited to write to the editorial director of Veloce at the above address. British Library Cataloguing in Publication Data – A catalogue record for this book is available from the British Library. Design and production by Veloce. Printed and bound in the UK by Short Run Press Ltd.

LOTUS CARS

1952 to 2024

A Pictorial History

Matthew Vale

CONTENTS

ACKNOWLEDGEMENTS

I would like to thank the following, without whom this book would not have happened. Firstly, Rob Ford of Club Lotus, who went above and beyond to find Club members – Jennie Lawrence and Andrew Wooley – willing to let me use pictures of their Elises.

I would also like to thank the other Lotus owners whose cars are featured here, and who have contributed to my other books on the marque. These include Brian Goodison, Jeff Boughton, Andrew Komosa, Melody and Henry Koslowski, Jon Bradbury, John Humfryes, Terry Stillman, Dave Groves, Roland Long, Malcolm Ricketts, Leigh Greenham, Royston Bing, Martin Bradbury and Martin Houston.

I'd also like to thank my long-suffering wife Julia, daughter Liz, and son in law Simon, for putting up with me writing yet another book.

Finally, I would like to dedicate this book to my granddaughter, Delphine.

An impressive display of Lotus VIs (above), and an assortment of Lotus Elan M100s at the Club Lotus Castle Combe track day in 2025.

A BRIEF HISTORY OF LOTUS

Introduction

Lotus has a long and illustrious history of producing both racing and road-going sports cars. This book guides the reader through the company's petrol engined, road-going sports car segment of that history, beginning with the Lotus VI. While the VI was ostensibly a competition car, it was road legal, and, as it was the car that really set Lotus on its path of producing road cars with a racing pedigree, it deserves its place here.

The book also covers the Elite, Seven, Elan, Plus 2, Europa, the new Elite, Éclat, and Esprit family, the new Elan M100, as well as the Elise, Exige and the Evora. Finally, it looks at those cars that, while not actually made by Lotus, had major input from the company with regard to their suspension and engines, and were often Lotus-badged as well.

It's widely acknowledged that Colin Chapman's main interest was racing. However, it was the road cars that generated the money that allowed him to pursue his many World Championships. To achieve the level of international success reached required Lotus to have invested a lot in innovative and exciting racing technology, gaining a great deal of experience along the way. This knowledge was also exploited to make the road cars lighter, faster, better handling, and arguably better looking than the rivals. Owners of Lotus road cars from the 1950s onwards shared the mystique of competition success in Formulas 1, 2 and 3, US Indy cars, Le Mans, and countless other international and club level events. The company's products were all steeped in racing technology, and the 1960s and 1970s vintage Sevens and Elans are still acknowledged to be some of the best handling and performing sports cars ever made.

Colin Chapman was very adept at exploiting rules and regulations for his designs and products in both the racing arena and with his road cars. While his exploits in producing engineering innovations in his racing cars are legendary, there was one major regulation that he exploited with his road cars up to the 1970s, and that was lack of Purchase Tax on cars sold in the UK as kits of parts. While

A rather nice looking Elise Series 2, seen at Castle Combe.

A fine display of Lotus cars at a Club Lotus Track day, also at Castle Combe. In the front is a lovely Elan Sprint in classic gold leaf livery.

Purchase Tax was levied on complete cars, the components that made up the complete car were not taxed. So while the level of tax on complete cars varied over the years, the savings a mechanically minded owner could make were significant if they built their car from components. This led to the growth of the kit car industry in the UK, and while there were various regulations applied to kits – for example you could not buy all the components from the same company – the benefits of avoiding tax were substantial.

However, when Purchase Tax in the UK was replaced with Value Added Tax (VAT) in 1973, both complete cars and components were taxed, closing the loophole and giving no financial incentive to sell cars in component form. This change could have been a disaster for Lotus, as it effectively wiped out the profit margin on the Elan and Europa, but Chapman embarked on a move upmarket with the new Elite and the exotic Esprit, and these cars would carry the company through some turbulent years.

The company went through several owners following Chapman's death in 1982, including GM, Bugatti and Proton, but today, with the might of Chinese car company Geely behind it, the company is looking forward to the electric age with confidence.

The start of it all – lockups, stables and Austin Sevens (1949 to 1959)

The origins of the Lotus Company can be traced to the late 1940s, when engineer and entrepreneur Colin Chapman started by building a pair of Austin Seven-based specials (retrospectively named the Lotus I and II) aimed at the trials sector (where cars are put through their paces and timed while tackling an off road course). These first two cars were built in the lock-up garages behind Chapman's then girlfriend Hazel's parents' house in Muswell Hill, North London. Trials were soon abandoned, however, and road racing quickly came to the fore when the Formula 750 series was launched in 1950.

When Chapman met two fellow Austin Seven enthusiasts, brothers Michael and

The second Lotus ever built, a trials car based on an Austin Seven and built by Colin Chapman in 1949. The car was used by Chapman and his wife to be, Hazel, in trials and speed tests, and later for circuit racing.

Nigel Allen, the trio joined forces, and, using the Allens' well equipped workshop at their parents' house at 104 Vallance Road, Alexandra Park in North London, the Lotus III was produced. Still Austin Seven-based, Chapman started road racing in earnest with the car, which made its first appearance at the Bristol Motor Club and Light Car Club meeting at Castle Combe circuit in May 1951, where Chapman took first place in the Formula 750 race.

On 1 January 1952 the Lotus Engineering Company was formed by Chapman and Michael Allen. The new company left the Allen's workshop and moved into the former stables at the back of Chapman's father's pub, the Railway Hotel, in Hornsey, North London. The company expanded in these premises, initially serving the Formula 750 racing community by tuning and overhauling Austin Seven engines, modifying Austin Seven chassis for racing, and producing hydraulic brake conversions. In 1952 the company produced its first car with a Chapman-designed chassis – the space framed Lotus VI.

The VI gave Lotus its first standard product, which was sold in kit form and was arguably the company's first true production road car. From then on Lotus went from strength to strength, producing small numbers of road and racing versions of its cars for sale, again usually in kit form, to help fund Chapman's racing ambitions.

The Lotus VI was the first Lotus car to be produced in any numbers. It was very much an enthusiast's car that could be driven to work during the week and used for competition at the weekends. This example dates from 1954.

Colin and Hazel were married in October 1954, and the company continued to expand. During these years at Hornsey, Lotus produced a variety of sports racing cars, culminating in the very successful Lotus Eleven of 1956, which featured a space frame chassis and light alloy body. These cars revealed Chapman's genius for making parts of his cars serve more than one purpose. For example, the light alloy transmission tunnel of the Lotus Eleven was a stressed member of the chassis, which meant fewer chassis tubes and less weight.

In 1957 Lotus moved up in the racing world and entered the Formula 2 class with the Lotus 12. The road cars were not neglected, though, with the Type 14 Elite coming to the market in the same year.

The Elite departed from the successful Lotus formula of a tubular space frame with a lightly stressed alloy body to a radical design of glass fibre monocoque with minimal metal reinforcement.

Produced between 1957 and 1962 (although sales of unsold cars and body units from the factory continued for a further year or so) the Elite was not only bought by sporting owners as a fast and good handling GT car, it also raced successfully, and won its class at the Le Mans 24 Hours on a number of occasions.

The next road car produced by Lotus was

The Lotus Type 14 Elite was a GT car with the unique feature of a glass fibre monocoque bodyshell. Built from 1958 to 1962, the Elite was powered by a Coventry Climax engine.

The Elite was a very successful competition car, with many class wins at Le Mans. It is considered by many to be the prettiest car ever made.

The Lotus Seven was first produced in 1959 as a replacement for the Lotus VI. At the time of writing Caterham Cars was still producing cars based on this design.

the Lotus Seven: a minimalistic sports car with the traditional Lotus space frame chassis, minimal creature comforts, and, with very light weight, giving scintillating performance. The Seven was produced by Lotus from 1959 through to 1969, whereupon the rights to the design were then signed over to Caterham Cars, which, at the time of writing in 2025, was still producing the car.

As Lotus got more successful, it was running out of space and facilities on the Hornsey site, and so Chapman started looking for a new site to continue the company's success.

Expansion and credibility: Cheshunt Factory (1960 to 1966)

In 1959 Lotus left its Hornsey premises and moved to a purpose-built factory on a five-acre site in Delamere Road, Cheshunt. The site was just outside of London, with its restrictive planning and development rules, but was only around ten miles from Hornsey, so still within reach of Lotus' skilled employees. Chapman managed to buy a bigger plot than he needed and then sold half of it to give him the capital to design and build an all-new factory, the layout of which was rumoured to be based on the highly efficient Volkswagen plant at Wolfsburg. The site housed two side-by-side 9000ft^2 (836m^2) factory buildings, with a two-storey office block on the front of one.

One building was allocated to Lotus Engineering, which made the Lotus Seven and the racing cars and also housed Team Lotus, and the other was initially turned over to Lotus Elite assembly. The new factory gave the company the facilities it needed to expand production and grow. However, despite the new factory, production of the Elite was slow, and, with the bodyshells and engines being produced by outside contractors, profit margins were slim, if not non-existent. It was becoming obvious that if the company was to prosper it needed a new line in road cars to replace the Elite, and the new line had to be more profitable and easier

The Lotus Elan was a turning point for Lotus. It was a fast, light and agile sports car, powered by Lotus' own engine, the legendary Twin Cam. This is a Series 1 example.

and quicker to build. The outcome of this was the Elan.

The Elan came into existence thanks to a piece of inspired improvisation. After Chapman and designer Ron Hickman had struggled to produce an open-topped glass fibre monocoque, Hickman had designed a lightweight, easy to build backbone chassis using folded steel sheet to act as a buck to test the proposed suspension. It must have been a eureka moment for both Hickman and Chapman when the first suspension mule was tested. With a proprietary Falcon glass fibre body crudely adapted to fit the unconventional chassis, the test mule exhibited such outstanding performance and handling that the plans for a glass fibre monocoque were dropped, and the simple Elan body, which sat astride the new chassis, was swiftly designed.

The simple chassis was cheap to produce by an outside company, and the largely unstressed body could be easily made in-house, meaning that margins on the Elan could be much higher than on the Elite; the only issue was what could power the new car. The answer came from the Technical Director at *Autocar* magazine and ex-Coventry Climax and Jaguar engineer Harry Mundy.

Lotus commissioned Mundy to design a new twin camshaft cylinder head and timing cover, which could be bolted onto the new 1498cc Ford engine block used in the Anglia. The Anglia engine was designed in the 1950s and was a fully up-to-date short-stroke four-cylinder unit with five main bearings. Importantly the engine was available from Ford UK, and, thanks to Ford's economies of scale, it was cheap.

The all-new light alloy cylinder head and front timing cover simply bolted onto the standard Ford unit. With a slight increase in capacity to 1558cc thanks to new pistons and larger bores, and with a pair of twin-choke Weber carburettors, Lotus had a little firecracker of an engine that produced 105bhp.

This was the final part of the Elan jigsaw, resulting in a state-of-the-art sports car with giant-killing performance and handling, and which would go on to be Lotus' main road car into the 1970s, enabling the company to begin moving upmarket and also perform creditably on the race track.

The Elan entered production in 1963, and quickly established itself as the sports car to have. While its performance and handling fully justified its success, it is pertinent to note that under the bonnet there were virtually no elements of the Ford-sourced engine block visible; just the Lotus-branded cylinder head, new alloy timing case, and the sporting Weber carburettors.

A second asset in Lotus' road car armoury was the Lotus Cortina, which entered 'production' at Cheshunt in 1963. The Lotus Cortina came about thanks to Ford Director Walter Hayes, who was very much of the 'Win on Sunday, Sell on Monday' persuasion, and oversaw a massive injection of time and money into Ford motorsport. The Lotus

The last of the line for the Elan was the Series 4 Sprint. This is the coupé version, showing the two-tone paint finish often used on this model.

The Elan Plus 2 was a 2+2 version of the original Elan. Wider and longer, with room for a couple of kids in the back, it was all Elan under the skin. This is a rare John Player Special model, with its black and gold livery celebrating Lotus grand prix victories in 1972.

Cortina's success on the race track, it was intended, would promote Ford's family saloon range.

The Lotus Cortina had a Twin Cam engine, and, initially, a revised rear suspension layout with trailing arms and an 'A' frame, along with weight saving alloy bonnet, boot and door skins. Ford supplied white-painted shells, while Lotus built the cars at Cheshunt, and also added the distinctive green side stripe.

The success of the Elan and the Lotus Cortina was mirrored by the increasing success of the company's racing cars, many of which were now mid-engined to compete with the highly competitive Coopers.

The factory was not resting on its laurels, though; while the space frame chassis in the Type 24 was state of the art in 1962, and was winning races, in 1963 the factory introduced the revolutionary Type 25 monocoque body single-seater, which would win races all over Europe. Lotus was also making progress in the USA; a pair of monocoque chassis Type 29s powered by Ford V8s came second and seventh at the 1963 Indianapolis 500, and Lotus followed this up with a win in 1965 with the Type 38.

With production of the Elan increasing, the introduction of the Plus 2 and the new mid-engined Europa in the pipeline, the company was swiftly running out of space at its Cheshunt factory. Despite building a further factory unit on the site, there was no room left to expand. So, after only six years on the new site, Chapman began casting around for a new base; and his eyes turned to the east of the country.

More expansion and a new base: Hethel (1966 to date)

Lotus moved into the former World War Two bomber airfield site at Hethel in Norfolk in 1966, and is still there today. The new base meant that Lotus had a much bigger site, with some hangars, as well as the perimeter road that made a perfect test track, and an operational airfield that meant Chapman could indulge in his hobby of flying!

The new site provided plenty of room for the production of the Elan, Plus 2 and Europa

The Europa was Lotus' first mid-engined road car, its engine and gearbox from the Renault 16. The Series 1 cars, like this one, were originally for export to Europe and were all left-hand drive.

The final Europa model was the Twin Cam, which, as the name implies, was powered by the Lotus Twin Cam engine. These Lotus-powered Europas had the flying buttresses on each side of the engine cover cut down to improve visibility.

Lotus went upmarket with its new Elite of 1974. A four-seat, three-door hatchback aimed at the successful executive, the car was powered by Lotus' new 2-litre 900 series engine.

With the Elite, Lotus adopted 'wedge' styling, and the long roof and rear hatch gave rear seat passengers plenty of headroom. The styling was a bit too radical for some customers, and Lotus marketed a coupé version, the Éclat, alongside it.

The Excel took the Éclat's coupé style rear end, and, with revised mechanical components from Toyota, was a fast, reliable and comfortable 2+2 sports coupé.

The Lotus Esprit, a mid-engined coupé, was the sports car of the range during the '70s and '80s. The first models had razor sharp lines penned by Giorgetto Giugiaro of ItalDesign.

road cars, along with the successful racing cars.

With the introduction of VAT on car components in 1973, Lotus left the kit car market behind and moved upmarket. This resulted in the wedge-shaped Elite, introduced in 1974, a four-seat luxury sports car powered by Lotus' own 2-litre engine.

Having dropped the Elan and Plus 2 in 1973, and the Europa in 1974, the Elite and Éclat would be Lotus' main road cars through the 1970s, joined by the mid-engined Esprit in 1975. Lotus progressed through the late 1970s with this lineup until 1982 when Colin Chapman died. This threw the company into crisis, and, with loans being called in, things did not look good.

Chief Engineer Mike Kimberley took up the leadership, and managed, against the odds, to save the company, thanks to a major loan from Toyota. This was soon followed by the creation of a consortium with Toyota, British Car Auctions, and JCB, which controlled the company before General Motors (GM) stepped in and bought it in 1985. Despite the close ties with Toyota made during the early 1980s, which resulted in major improvements in reliability and engineering integrity, Lotus had to go to GM in 1986 for the powertrain for the new Elan M100 of 1989, and the collaboration

The last Lotus Esprits were restyled by Peter Stevens, and had softer lines than the earlier models. Here, the yellow Esprit from 2000 sits between its stablemates, two Elan M100s.

The Elan M100 was a front-wheel drive open-topped two-seater, powered by an Isuzu engine. Introduced in 1989 it was acclaimed by the press for its handling prowess, but the car was not a commercial success.

The Elise was introduced in 1995 and went on sale in 1996. This is Andrew Wooley's 1998 example and shows off the car's clean and innovative lines.

also led to the tarmac-burning Lotus Carlton of 1990.

GM's tenure came to an end in 1993 when Lotus was sold to Bugatti, then owned by Romano Artioli. The replacement for the Elan was conceived at this point, with the design of the car that would be first seen in the flesh as the Elise launched in 1995. The Elise proved that Lotus had not lost its mojo; it remained in production in various guises until 2021, and also spawned the Vauxhall/Opel VX220 sports car of 2000.

In 1997 Lotus changed hands again, this time being sold to Malaysian manufacturer Proton. Mike Kimberley returned in 2005, and was appointed CEO in 2006, whereupon

The Lotus Elise had an aluminium platform chassis and glass fibre bodywork. Lightweight and agile, with fine performance and handling, it was a true successor to the original Elan.

To the left is a Series 2 Elise produced between 2000 and 2011, and to the right a Series 3 Elise from 2017.

he oversaw the introduction of a new flagship 2+2 sports model: the Evora. When Kimberley retired in 2009, Lotus seemed to lose its way, with much effort being devoted to marketing rather than actual projects, and no actual new cars coming to the market.

Production of the Elise Series 3 finally ended in 2021. This is Jennie Lawrence's 2019 example.

In 2017 the company was sold to Chinese car company Geely. The mid-engined Emira was announced in 2021 as the last Lotus to be powered by an internal combustion engine, and went on sale in 2022 as a replacement for the Evora, Exige and Elise. The company is now concentrating on designing and producing electric vehicles, including the Emeya, a four-door 'Hyper-GT' car, and the the Eletre SUV.

The Lotus Exige was a sport-oriented version of the Elise with a fixed roof. A notable feature of the car is the engine air intake on the roof.

The Evora was introduced in 2006 as a new top of the range 2+2 GT car. Larger than the Elise, and powered by a Toyota V6 engine, it was a state-of-the-art supercar.

The Emira is the last petrol-engined car to be produced by Lotus, and replaced the Evora and Elise. A true two-seater sports car, the Emira is a fitting end to Lotus' 70+ years of producing petrol-engined sports cars.

THE EARLY ROAD CARS – FROM THE VI TO THE ELITE

Produced in small numbers, the early Lotus road cars relied heavily on the company's racing experience, and were usually produced in kit form for enthusiastic owners to build. The VI was the first model that Lotus produced in any quantity, and was intended for both road and track use. With the VI, Lotus set itself on the path that Chapman originally mapped out: to produce road cars that would finance his racing ambitions.

The VI was followed by the Seven Elite, which eschewed the tubular steel space frame and instead used a glass fibre monocoque shell. The Elite was designed as a GT car, with one eye firmly on competition in endurance racing. The company was nothing if not innovative; the VI and the Seven were both state-of-the-art when they were introduced, with their space frame chassis; while the Elite's glass fibre monocoque was almost unique, and the car was good enough to win its class at Le Mans several years in succession. These early cars are rare and valuable, but with the production of the Seven being passed to Caterham Cars, it's perfectly possible to buy a new or used example of the Caterham Seven for a pretty reasonable sum.

The Lotus VI (1952 to 1955)

The Lotus VI was the first 'production' car produced by the young company in 1952. The VI was the first car to use a Lotus chassis, designed by Colin Chapman, and was aimed at the enthusiastic owner who would use the car for transport during the week and competition at the weekends. The VI was a simple car, with a light multi-tube space frame chassis, minimal light alloy bodywork, and exposed wheels (usually protected by separate cycle-type mudguards). The core

This Lotus VI was the first of the breed with the chassis number VI-1, and was first registered in 1952. It was raced by Colin Chapman and powered by a Ford Prefect engine.

Pictured at the British Motor Museum in Gaydon in 2013, the first Lotus VI shows off its Ford split axle front suspension, twin SU carburettors with their velocity stacks poking through the bonnet, and the twin headlamps lurking in the air intake.

The first Lotus VI was simple and businesslike. The tubular space frame construction is visible from the cockpit, and the instrument panel is comprehensive with the all important rev counter directly in front of the driver.

The Lotus VI had aluminium bodywork, which fully enclosed the rear wheels, while the fronts had to make do with lightweight motorcycle-style guards. This 1954 car was pictured at a Club Lotus track day at Castle Combe circuit.

of the car was the Lotus-supplied multi-tube space frame chassis, with stressed aluminium panels riveted to the floor and scuttle, and which was reported to weigh a mere 55lb (25kg). The basic kit came with the chassis, plus a radiator (usually a modified Morris Minor unit), the pedals, a windscreen and frame, the handbrake and gear levers, a hood and frame or tonneau cover, and the upholstered seats.

The rest of the bodywork, comprising the driver and passenger cowl, the bonnet, nose cone, and the side and rear panels, were all available separately. The owner would present their own engine, gearbox, and the front and rear axles, and these would then be modified by Lotus to fit. The front suspension used a Chapman-designed 'split beam' conversion of the Ford solid front axle to give semi-independent movement, and used combined coil spring over damper units. Steering was by the standard Ford worm and gear steering box made by Burman. At the rear the live axle was sprung using combined coil over damper units, as seen on the front end, and was located laterally by a Panhard rod.

Various proprietary engines, gearboxes and final drives were chosen and fitted by the purchasers, and were inevitably budget and availability dependent. There was, therefore, no standard specification for the car, and most of the 110 or so produced between 1952 and 1955 were unique. What was common was the car's chassis and its

This late Lotus VI in polished alloy shows the model's lightweight front mudguards and the neat split front axle giving independent front suspension.

Simple lines with no unnecessary adornments are hallmarks of the Lotus VI. Designed to be at home on the track, the car could be, and was, used on the road by hardy owners.

light weight, good handling and sporting performance. Engine options ranged from pedestrian Ford side-valve units, via the easy-to-tune BMC 'A' series, to out-and-out race units from the likes of Coventry Climax and its FW light alloy overhead-camshaft, fire pump-derived, four-cylinder units. Production of the VI ceased in 1955 after about 110 cars had been produced.

Lotus VI specification

ENGINE: Various, including Ford side-valve 1172 and Ford Consul 1500, BMC A Series, MG TF, and Coventry Climax FWA.
GEARBOX: Various.
SUSPENSION: Front: Modified Ford axle giving split-beam semi-independent system. Combined coil spring and damper units. **Rear:** Live rear axle with combined coil spring and damper units and Panhard rod.
STEERING: Burman worm and ball type (from the Ford Popular).
BRAKES: Drums all round.
WHEELS AND TYRES: Various.
DIMENSIONS: Length: 121in (307.3cm); **width:** 51in (129.5cm); **track front:** 49in (124.5cm); **track rear:** 45in (114.3cm); **height:** (to scuttle top) 30.5in (77.47cm); **wheelbase:** 87-90in (221-228.6cm).
WEIGHT: 952lb (431kg).
PERFORMANCE: Dependent on engine.

The Lotus Seven (1957 to 1973)

The Lotus Seven was a logical replacement for the VI but its introduction was delayed until 1957 as the development of the first Elite took precedence. Usually offered in kit form, the Seven was supplied with all-new components, including the engine and gearbox, which was unusual for the kit car market at the time. However, this also meant that a buyer would need to buy the car from two separate Lotus companies, enabling the purchase to be exempt from Purchase Tax.

The Seven was launched alongside the Lotus Type 14 Elite at the 1957 Earls Court Motor Show in London. Unlike the Elite, the Seven was ready to go to customers, and was an immediate success, with traditional Lotus buyers looking for what was, in effect, an updated and modernised replacement for the VI. The car was a competitive club racer, and could be used on the road, with hardier drivers using them as their daily driver. It had been under development since 1955 when the 'Seven' name had been assigned, but sat on the back burner until it finally emerged. While keeping to the ethos of a road legal but competition-oriented car, the Seven switched the VI's ethos of being a competition car that could be used on the road, to a road

This early Seven has wire wheels and a roll cage, and maintains the family resemblance to the previous Lotus VI.

The Seven in stripped back racing specification is very much a competition machine. The design had evolved from the Lotus VI but still displays a certain purposeful look.

One of the major differences between the Seven and the Lotus VI was the front suspension. The Seven had a fully independent double wishbone setup, as seen here.

car that could be used for competition. By downplaying the competition aspects of the car but still keeping it basic and light, Lotus increased the potential market for it.

This meant the car's specification still appealed to competition-oriented owners who bought the VI, but also appealed to enthusiasts who wanted a road car with sparkling performance, although not using the car for serious competition. However, the Seven made few concessions to comfort and usability, and remains to this day an uncompromising performance-oriented machine.

The kits were built by Lotus Components, effectively the Lotus race shop, and their manufacture was fitted in around the production of the then current range of Lotus competition machinery, namely the Elite and early Elan, plus the racing cars.

This 1961 Seven is fitted with the classic racing 'Wobbly Web' wheels. These early cast alloy wheels were a common racing fitment in the 1950s and '60s. The side screens offered some weather protection for the driver and passenger.

As already mentioned, the car was usually supplied in kit form, and customers could choose whether to buy the mechanical parts directly from Lotus or source them elsewhere. Alternatively, they could buy a completely built up car, but this meant the price was inflated by the dreaded (and at times punitive) Purchase Tax.

With the Seven, Lotus retained the basis of the VI's tubular space frame chassis, but enhanced it using riveted-on alloy sheets to add strength and rigidity, and to simplify the chassis construction. The car also featured under-shields for the engine bay and rear end made from light alloy sheet. Both round and square section tubing was used to build the welded chassis, and, with the riveted-on alloy body panels, provided a stiff and well triangulated structure.

Initially, the use of glass fibre, soon to become a Lotus 'trademark', was limited to the stylish nose cone, while double curvature body panels in alloy covered the sides and rear of the car. Front mudguards were alloy cycle-type, and the rear guards, also made from light alloy, hugged the bodywork.

Keeping with the VI's spartan layout of two seats, no doors and front 'cycle wings', the Seven was fitted out with minimal seats and red plastic trim, and could be supplied with optional weather equipment comprising clip-on side screens and a hood that had to be physically 'built' in place providing a basic level of weather protection. Mind you, the weather gear predicated the ordering of the bolt-on, full-width windscreen that was also an option. Hardy owners made do with an aero screen and speed to keep off the rain ...

From the rear this 1964 Seven shows off the integrated rear mudguards, and a tonneau cover to keep out the rain.

At the front was a Lotus-designed twin-wishbone front suspension setup taken from the Series 2 Lotus Eleven, and the car used Triumph Mayflower drum brakes along with a Burman steering box. The latter was rapidly changed for a Morris Minor steering rack (which was mounted upside down), and by 1959 a Triumph Herald steering rack was fitted. A Lotus specification spring over damper unit joined the lower wishbone to the chassis; the system performed well and proved largely trouble-free as long as the lower trunnions were kept lubricated. If things

With a side exiting exhaust and Wobbly Web wheels this 1961 Seven is set up for racing and fast road use. There is limited luggage space under the tonneau cover behind the seats.

did go wrong, parts were cheap and readily available.

At the rear there was a live axle from Austin, which was sprung using coil springs with separate dampers, and trailing links secured the axle fore and aft. Engines were initially Ford's side-valve 100E unit as used in the Anglia, with a three-speed gearbox. Lotus offered tuning kits to raise the power of the old side-valve unit from a standard 30bhp to a heady 40bhp, and customers could also specify a close-ratio gearbox. In 1958, the year after the car's launch, Lotus offered the option of a Coventry Climax FW engine creating the Super Seven and later Seven C models. The standard car with the somewhat asthmatic Ford engine was renamed the Seven E. In 1959 the Seven A was introduced, with a BMC A Series engine and BMC four-speed gearbox from the Austin A30/Morris Minor. The A series produced 37bhp as standard, but was very tunable and much more modern than the Ford unit. The Series 1 Seven was introduced in 1957 and was produced until 1960.

Lotus Seven Series 1 specification

ENGINE: Various, including Ford side-valve 1172 and Ford Consul 1500, BMC A Series, MG TF and Coventry Climax FWA.
GEARBOX: Various.
SUSPENSION: Front: Independent, twin wishbones, coil over damper; **rear:** Live rear axle with combined coil spring and damper units.
STEERING: Rack and pinion.
BRAKES: Drums all round, diameter 8in (20.32cm).
WHEELS AND TYRES: Steel, 15in bolt-on, 5.20x15.
DIMENSIONS: Length: 129in (327.6cm); **width:** 53in (134.6cm); **track front:** 47in (119.4cm); **track rear:** 46in (116.8cm); **height:** 28in (71.1cm); **wheelbase:** 88in (223.5cm).
WEIGHT: 950lb (430.9kg).
PERFORMANCE: Dependent on engine.

The Lotus Seven Series 1 was superseded by the Series 2, introduced in 1960 and produced up to 1968 (a relatively long production run). The main purpose of the Series 2 was to simplify construction and thus cut costs, so it had a new chassis and the Coventry Climax engine option was canned. The chassis was redesigned to simplify construction and reduce the amount of material used, and the light alloy flooring of the engine bay and rear end was omitted. A Standard 10 axle was specified, with its location simplified by the use of a single trailing arm to each side and a single upper, which had the effect of standardising the wheel stud centres. Triumph Herald 13in wheels were adopted all round. The light alloy cycle-type front mudguards used on the Series 1 were replaced with long sweeping glass fibre items that would become a Seven characteristic, and the Series 1's bodywork was simplified, still using alloy sheets but losing most of the difficult-to-produce double curvature. Being glass fibre rather than alloy, the rear mudguards were now cheaper to produce.

On this 1961 Seven the spare wheel is mounted on the rear of the bodywork, and the neat shallow instrument panel can be seen.

The Series 2 was initially powered by either a Ford 100E with the three-speed gearbox, or BMC A Series engine with four-speed BMC gearbox; both as used on the later Series 1 cars. In 1961 the Ford 105E overhead valve unit with its four-speed gearbox was made available. This over-square short-stroke unit could rev a lot more freely than the A Series unit, and replaced the 100E unit option.

By 1967 marketing and development of the Seven had been devolved to Graham Neame's Caterham Cars, the sole distributor of the Seven. The Series 3 was produced from 1968 through to 1970, and could be

The Series 2 Seven was introduced in 1960. This 1963 example has the long sweeping glass fibre front wings, which were a standard feature and gave the car a more modern look.

With glass fibre replacing aluminium, the Series 2 Seven rear mudguards were cheaper to produce and were painted. The new front wings gave better weather protection, and the shallow luggage space behind the cabin can be seen.

Ready to hit the Castle Combe circuit is this 1964 Seven Series 2. The sparse lines of the car were enhanced by the new front mudguards.

Some Series 2 Sevens were painted overall – this rather nice example from 1963 is in Lotus Yellow. Note the side screens still in place.

This Series 3 Lotus Seven has had custom made aluminium mudguards fitted, front and rear. With its stunning polished finish, the car is a credit to its owner.

The Series 3 is normally all body coloured. This promotional shot shows the factory standard Dunlop alloy wheels and the Lotus Yellow paint.

powered by a standard Ford Crossflow 225E or a Holby-tuned Crossflow engine. The old Standard 10 axle was replaced with a Ford Escort Mexico unit, as this could handle the ever increasing power from the 225E engine, and the wheels were enlarged to 5½J units as seen on the Lotus Cortina. The Holby-tuned 225E had a pair of twin-choke Weber carburettors, a hotter camshaft, and a new and less restrictive exhaust manifold. In this form the unit produced around 84bhp, and was named by Holby as its CFR unit.

The driver's needs were not forgotten: the Series 3 gained an external fuel filler to replace the cabin-mounted one in the Series 2, and, for the first time on the Seven, it sported a fuel gauge in the dash – prior to this owners relied on a notched stick to estimate how much fuel they had! Black upholstery replaced the previous red.

After much customer demand Lotus eventually shoehorned a Lotus Twin Cam engine into the Seven, creating the Series 3 Twin Cam SS. This car had a Holby-tuned Twin Cam engine producing 124bhp, and the chassis was modified to resist the increased power. The dash was changed to an engraved aluminium item, the car was properly carpeted, and had flush-mounted rear lights and a new slatted grille. There was a considerable price premium over the standard car, and only around 13 were built during 1969.

The Series 4 was introduced in March 1969 to replace the Series 3. This was an all-new design, but very much in the spirit of the original Seven. A new simplified chassis was designed that mixed tubular construction with sheet steel sides for the cockpit and engine bay, and a folded sheet steel front

The Lotus Seven Series 4 was a very different beast from the previous cars, but still retained the Seven look. This brochure shot shows the new front end.

crossmember. All-new glass fibre bodywork was longer and wider, with a full-width rear end enclosing the wheels and longer Series 3 style front wings stretching back to the rear mudguards. As Ford had replaced the 105E engine with the new crossflow 225E unit, in 1598cc and 1297cc capacities, these two engines were the only 'factory' options, and both came with the Ford four-speed gearbox.

The car's interior was wider, giving more elbow room for the driver and passenger, while the whole interior was new, with better seats and a new dashboard. For the Series 4's bodywork, glass fibre replaced most of the alloy panels used on the Series 3, cutting costs. The Series 4 featured a much more enveloping glass fibre body tub, which gave it a more integrated look, but lost much of the earlier car's timeless simplicity. The sweeping front wings of the previous models were retained, and, with the wider cockpit, the car looked much more modern. The update did not extend to proper doors or

The more integrated lines of the Series 4 Seven can be seen in this brochure shot. It is obvious why most Sevens of any series are usually seen without the hood in place – the factory assembly seen here is not one of the most elegant soft tops.

side windows, but the removable side panels now had sliding perspex windows to add a small amount of practicality. A hardtop was available from the factory, but was rarely specified.

Lotus stopped building the Seven in 1973. The Series 4 had not been the sales success it deserved to be, and with the imminent imposition of Value Added Tax on all goods – including car parts and components as well as complete cars – the tax savings in purchasing a kit car disappeared. Lotus then sold the rights to the Seven to Graham Neame's Caterham Cars, the sole distributor, which began producing the cars in-house. Production began with the then current Series 4, but quickly reverted to offering a lightly modified Series 3 – it was more of a purist's car and one that appealed to the hardcore Seven enthusiasts more than the heavier and less popular Series 4.

Probably the most famous Lotus Seven is the 1965 Series 2 KAR120C, used by actor Patrick McGoohan as agent number 6 In the cult TV series *The Prisoner*. Before his incarceration the secret agent's main mode of transport was the Lotus – possibly not the most inconspicuous mode of transport for someone who was supposed to be a secret agent.

Lotus Seven Series 4 specification

ENGINE: Ford Crossflow, 1300cc or 1600cc straight four, with pushrod-operated overhead valves. Power dependent on state of tune.
GEARBOX: Ford Corsair, four-speed.
SUSPENSION: Front: Independent, twin wishbones, coil over damper; **rear:** Live rear axle with combined coil spring and damper units and four links.
STEERING: Rack and pinion.
BRAKES: Front: 9in (22.8cm) discs; **rear:** 8in (20.3cm) diameter.
WHEELS AND TYRES: 13x5.5 alloy, 165SR13 tyres.
DIMENSIONS: Length: 146.3in (370.8cm); **width:** 60.5in (153.67cm); **track front:** 48.8in (123.95cm); **track rear:** 51.5in (130.8cm); **height:** 44in (111.76cm); **wheelbase:** 91in (231.14cm).
WEIGHT: 1310lb (594.21kg).

The Lotus Type 14 Elite (1959 to 1963)

The Lotus Type 14 Elite was an extremely pretty and well proportioned two-door coupé, and was Lotus' first true GT car. Designed to be 'a racing car for the road' (to quote model expert Denis Ortenburger), in pretty much standard form the car won its class (the under 1300cc Grand Touring) at Le Mans in 1959, 1960, 1961, 1962, 1963 and 1964; quite an impressive record. It also featured highly in the 'Index of Thermal Efficiency' class. The Elite's success was not just at Le Mans; in its first race in the 1958 Autosport Series-Production Sports Car Championships the Elite won the 1600cc class, and ruled the roost in the small-engined GT classes over the following years.

The Elite has an unmatched record of competition success, and is still being raced competitively in historic events today. It featured an innovative all glass fibre monocoque chassis that provides great strength, lightness and rigidity, and the lightweight all-alloy Coventry Climax engine gave it superlative performance despite a capacity of only 1200cc.

The final part of the winning specification was the car's long-travel, softly sprung, all round independent suspension that guaranteed excellent and largely problem-free handling and roadholding.

The front suspension had a fairly conventional arrangement on each side, with a single top link and anti-roll bar, and a wide angled bottom wishbone. The top link ran at 90 degrees to the car's centre line, the anti-roll bar formed the second top wishbone, and was connected to the outer end of the link by a rubber bush and ran forwards across the front of the car to connect up with the top link on the other side. The lower wishbone's rear arm ran parallel to the top link, while the forward arm was angled at about 45 degrees to a mount on the front of the body. The steering rack was mounted behind the suspension, and operated on an arm on the rear of the upright. The brake calliper was mounted on the rear of the upright.

The rear suspension was unique and innovative. It used the drive shaft and a trailing

These two pictures show a prototype Elite from 1959, believed to be the Geneva Motor Show car of that year. When pictured it was owned by Roland Long, who commissioned the car's restoration.

arm to locate the wheel in the horizontal plane (ie fore and aft), while a 'Chapman Strut' – a combined spring and damper unit – located the wheel in the vertical plane (ie up and down). The early cars used a single cranked trailing arm to locate the hub, which was bolted to the body forward of the hub, while later cars had a two-armed 'twisted wishbone' trailing arm that had the two arms bolted to the bottom of the hub and a single forward mount on the body. The wheel hub itself was integral with the suspension unit, and carried the bearing for the drive shaft that ran through the hub. The result was a suspension system with relatively long wheel travel, was controlled using soft springs and carefully calculated firm damping, giving the car superlative handling and roadholding.

The braking system was unusual for the day, with discs all round when most road cars had all drums, and only some so called 'sports cars' had disc brakes up front. The Elite's front and rear discs were 9.5in (24.1cm) in diameter, and were gripped by two-piston callipers made by Girling. The rear discs were mounted inboard, close to the differential to maximise unsprung weight at the expense of accessibility; unlike some other sports cars the Elite did not seem to suffer from the inboard rear brakes overheating which was probably down to their relatively large size and the car's low weight.

The wheels were lightweight 15in diameter, 48-spoke, knock-on units with splined hubs, and tyres were 4.80x15 crossply.

As well as the car's innovative and sophisticated suspension, the power unit was also state-of-the-art. The Coventry Climax engine that, in various sizes, was used across many racing classes, was born from the UK Government requirement for an engine to power a new prototype fire pump for the British Civil Defence Organisation at the start of the cold war, when the threat of a nuclear attack from the Soviet Block was all too real. The result was a little gem of an engine – a four-cylinder unit with a light alloy crankcase and cylinder head, with a single chain-driven overhead camshaft operating two valves per cylinder. Importantly the engine was designed to run at maximum revs from startup, and to continue running for potentially hours (if not days). The engine was integrated into a portable pump unit that could be carried easily by two men. When displayed at the October 1953 Earls Court Motor Show in London its potential for car use was obvious, and racing versions of the engine soon appeared.

The first automotive version of the fire pump engine was the 1097cc FWA unit, which became available to car makers in 1955, and fell within the 1100cc racing class. This unit had bore and stroke measurements of 72.4mm by 66.6mm, and with a compression ratio of 9.8:1 produced 76bhp. Following on from the FWA was the FWB, which was aimed at the 1500cc racing class. With bore and stroke of 76.2 x 80mm the FWB displaced 1460cc, and with a compression ratio of 11:1 produced 108bhp.

The Elite was aimed at the 1300cc racing class so its engine would have to sit between these two variants of the fire pump unit. The FWE engine then came about by combining the cylinder block (and hence the bore) of the FWB, and the crankshaft (and hence the stroke) of the FWA. The FWE thus had a bore and stroke of 76.2 x 66.6mm, giving a capacity of 1216cc. This marriage of parts gave an engine that used a large number of Coventry Climax's production components, and the first 500 or so engines were fitted with a single carburettor, a cast iron exhaust

The Lotus Elite is owned by Lotus enthusiast Malcolm Ricketts and is a 1961 Series 2 model. The yellow paint contrasts nicely with the metalic silver roof.

Under the bonnet of the Elite sits a little gem of an engine: the all-alloy Coventry Climax FWE – the Feather Weight Elite unit. Displacing a mere 1216cc the unit produced up to 100bhp and powered the Elite to many class wins at Le Mans.

manifold, and, with a 10:1 compression ratio, produced a healthy 75bhp. Later engines with twin carburettors produced up to 105bhp. The all alloy construction of the FWE engine meant it was very light – in twin carb form the engine weighed a mere 215lb (97.5kg). For comparison, the Lotus Twin Cam unit used in the Elan weighed around 290lb (131.5kg).

The main innovation displayed by the Elite was its glass fibre monocoque chassis. While not the first car to use the new super-material to make a chassis, the Elite's bodyshell had a minimum of steel reinforcement, and can be accurately described as a true glass fibre monocoque. The application of science also meant that the Elite chassis was properly stressed with the properties of glass fibre reinforced plastic (grp) taken into account in the design – it was not a steel monocoque remade in glass fibre. Lotus utilised the properties of the new material to provide a chassis that was both light and strong, with reliability and durability while minimising weight.

The body design was centred around defining the loads to which the body was subject, and confining those loads into well understood structures – basically a series of grp torsion boxes positioned around a single transverse bulkhead. While a grp structure has between one eighth to one third the tensile strength of a steel structure, and weighs about one fifth, a grp structure can be easily reinforced by adding layers at critical areas so it was possible to produce a much lighter structure that was just as stiff and strong as a steel one. The Elite's bodyshell was properly stressed by Chapman, making sure the body was as light and stiff as possible. The structural boxes that gave the car its strength were fully integrated into the body design as follows.

One box was sited transversely at the front of the car, and was joined to a pair of longitudinal boxes sited behind the front wheels. The latter two boxes were joined together by a transverse box that formed the scuttle bulkhead. The passenger 'cell' was formed from two sill boxes, the central transmission tunnel, and a double-skinned box that formed the cell's roof. These central boxes were joined to the front bulkhead and to a second rear box that formed the rear bulkhead and carried the differential and the rear suspension pickups.

There were two metal structures glassed into the monocoque. At the front was a steel framework, bonded to the front two longitudinal boxes, that provided the pickup points for the front suspension and engine mounts. In the centre of the car, extending from the front of the sills, up the A pillars, and around the windscreen was a tubular hoop

This 1963 Elite S2, owned by Terry Stillman, shows off its lovely silver over dark blue paintwork in the summer sun. With its chromed wire wheels and minimal bodywork adornments the purity of the Elite's design shines through.

that reinforced the windscreen opening, and provided a single jacking point on each side of the car.

The only downside of the body design was noise – the car was subject to a certain amount of criticism at the time as it wasn't the quietest on the road, with a lot of road and mechanical noise heard in the cabin. Initially, the bodyshells were produced by Miramar, a boat building company, and the first bodies sometimes had problems, mainly around the differential mountings, which could pull out of the shell under stress. This was found to be due to the manufacturer not conforming to the original design. Later bodies, from around no 278 and from 1960 onwards, were produced by Bristol, and were considered to be much better quality.

The Elite's stylish looks were created by Peter Kirwan-Taylor, a Lotus customer and friend of Colin Chapman. The Elite's interior was relatively conventional, if somewhat sparse. The two seats were positioned either side of the large transmission tunnel 'box', and most of the space behind the seats was taken up by the horizontally mounted spare wheel. The dashboard was a neat design that mimicked the Elite's profile with its slightly

This 1963 Elite was photographed at Goodwood at the 81st Members Meeting. A fitting place for an Elite to be, bearing in mind the car's outstanding competition history.

exaggerated length, housing the instruments in the central 'cabin' area, with the minor switches appearing each in the lower 'bonnet' and 'boot' depictions. There were small fixed quarter lights at the front of the doors, and the main side windows were fixed, but could be removed entirely if required. Sound proofing was pretty much non-existent, and hence the interior of the car could be noisy as the bodyshell was prone to uncomfortable 'booming' at certain speeds and engine revs.

With Lotus having moved to its new factory in Cheshunt, the first new Elite was sold on the 11th of March 1959. Production continued until about 1076 cars were completed during 1963. The cars with Miramar-produced bodies were retrospectively named the Series 1, while Bristol-bodied cars were all Series 2. The Elite was offered in standard or SE specifications, with the SEs having tuned engines with twin SU carbs and hotter cams. In the final year of production the factory offered a further series of performance models: the Super 95, Super 100 and Super 105. These were fitted with a pair of Weber twin-choke carbs, with the number representing the claimed power output of the progressively hotter engines.

The Elite was a major milestone for Lotus. It was its first road-going GT car, had a very impressive competition record, and, with over 1000 produced, was the important leap that led to Lotus becoming recognised as a car manufacturer in its own right. It also taught Lotus some important lessons on how to run a car business. Aside from reinforcing the need for proper design and testing processes, probably the most important lesson was how to make money from building a car. It has been reported that Lotus made very little if any profits from the Elite. The car was expensive and time-consuming to build, and with most of the major components – notably the bodyshell and the drivetrain – being produced by outside manufacturers, the margins on the car must have been slim as the suppliers were taking their profits from the parts they supplied to

The purposeful look of this 1963 Elite is accentuated by the racing accoutrements: the bonnet catches, lack of bumpers, taped headlamps and racing number roundel all imply some racing heritage.

The inside of the Elite is attractive and well fitted out. Opinions differ as to whether the shape of the dash was designed to mirror the car's profile, but either way it is a unique and attractive piece of work.

The Elite is probably the best looking car ever made. This is Malcolm Ricketts' Series 2 car basking in the sunshine.

Lotus. However, Chapman was a quick learner, and in the Elite's replacement, the Elan, the company was to build its own bodyshell and engine, which meant that the margins were kept in house and the Elan actually made Lotus money. However, the economics should not cloud the fact that the Elite was a very impressive car in its own right, and, with its record of wins at Le Mans and elsewhere, was one of the most successful road-going racing cars ever.

Lotus Elite specification

ENGINE: Coventry Climax FWE, straight-four, all alloy, single overhead camshaft, light alloy head and block, single (75bhp) or twin (80bhp) SU carburettors.
GEARBOX: BMC four-speed, optional ZF five-speed.
SUSPENSION: Front: Independent with single upper link and anti-roll bar, wide spaced lower wishbone. Combined spring and damper units. **Rear:** Independent with trailing arm and Chapman struts (combined coil spring and damper units). Load bearing drive shafts.
STEERING: Rack and pinion.
BRAKES: 9.5in (24.1cm) discs front and rear. Twin-piston callipers.
WHEELS AND TYRES: 15in knock-on 48-spoke wire wheels; **tyres:** 4.80x15.
DIMENSIONS: Length: 130in (330.2cm); **width:** 58in (147.3cm); **track front and rear:** 47in (119.4cm); **height:** 46in (116.8cm); **wheelbase:** 88in (223.5cm).
WEIGHT: 1512lb (685.8kg).
PERFORMANCE: Top speed: 120mph (193kph); **0-60:** 10.6 seconds.

A PLETHORA OF ELANS AND A PLUS 2 FOR THE FAMILY

The Lotus Elan was the car that marked Lotus' move from manufacturing quirky, niche racing oriented cars to mainstream performance cars. The Elan pioneered the formula for all Lotus cars up to the Elise: a lightweight glass fibre body sitting on a simple backbone chassis or subframe.

Combine this with a perky, powerful Twin Cam engine and a properly designed independent suspension, and Lotus' new small sports car was guaranteed to have great performance and outstanding handling. With these characteristics the Elan built a brilliant and enduring reputation for the Lotus brand. The Elan also had an important bonus for Lotus: not only did it out-perform and out-handle most of the competition, but it was also economical to make and was sold at a profit.

Probably the most famous Elan of all time – this is Jim Clark's S1 Elan now fully restored.

The heart of the Elan is its pressed sheet steel chassis, or subframe. The chassis is light, stiff and cheap to make, and it meant the glass fibre body was largely unstressed.

Lotus Type 26: Elan Series 1 and 2 (1962 to 1966)

In 1962 Lotus unveiled its replacement for the Type 14 Elite. The Elan was cheaper, simpler, and easier to manufacture than the Elite, and would prove to be Lotus' first really viable road car. It would also establish Lotus as a leading contender in the small sports car market. In the UK the Elan was available in kit form or fully assembled – if the prospective owner opted for the kit they saved having to pay the Purchase Tax due on a new car. So, in 1963 in kit form the car was £1095, and fully assembled £1499. Compare this with the price of more traditional fare – £949 for an MGB or £1032 for a TR4 and the importance of being offered a kit comes into perspective.

The Elan was different from the opposition. It was powered by Lotus' own engine, a state-of-the-art twin overhead camshaft engine breathing through a pair of exotic twin-choke Weber carbs from Italy. Its cylinder head was cast from lightweight alloy, and if you opened the bonnet there was no sign of the humble origins of the cast iron bottom end sourced from the unassuming Ford Anglia. Even so, this block utilised Ford's state-of-the-art iron block casting processes that resulted in very rigid and strong iron blocks, and it had a massively rigid bottom end with five main bearings.

The Lotus Twin Cam engine has gained legendary status for its strength, reliability and tuneability, and forms the heart of the Elan and its derivatives. One quirk of the design was that the inlet manifold was cast with the cylinder head. This meant modifications to the head casting were required when Stromberg carburettors were used. The provision of its own engine meant Lotus moved from being a producer of chassis and bodies, like TVR and Marcos, to being a car manufacturer in its own right. In the Series 1 Elan the engine produced 105bhp.

Under the Elan's bonnet sits the classic Lotus Twin Cam engine. While based on the Ford 1500's bottom end, the Lotus engine, with its double overhead camshafts and twin Weber carburettors, was state of the art for the time.

The Elan's all glass fibre bodyshell was hand-produced using a layup process. The

The first of the Elans was just right. The car epitomised form following function, with neat lines and no extra adornments or frivolities. This is Paddy Byres' Series 1.

The neat lines of the Elan Series 1 can be appreciated from this rear view. Note the individual round rear lights, and how the boot lid is recessed into the body.

From the front the Series 1 Elan shows off its glass fibre bumper and signature pop-up headlights.

bodyshell was constructed in two parts: a one-piece outer shell made in bolt-together moulds, which allowed for the 'tumblehome' evident on the neatly styled body's lower edges; and an inner shell forming the floor and engine bay. The two parts were then bonded together to form a stiff but light unit. The only structural metal used in the bodyshell was in the sill cavities and the A and B pillars, where a U-shaped latticework made from solid steel rod (actually the same type of rod used to reinforce concrete structures) was bonded into the body and supplemented the effect of the sills, to stop the shell folding up due to the absence of a roof.

The body also had small, light alloy 'bobbins' glassed in various places. These were drilled and used to mount such parts as the doors and boot lid onto the shell, and also to provide strength to the point where the body was bolted to the chassis or subframe. The doors had an unusually wide opening, with the hinge close to the edge of the front wheelarch, giving the driver and passenger easy access or exit from the cockpit.

Made from an inner and outer moulding, the doors had simple lift-up frameless windows operated via a chromed tang on the top of the glass. The bonnet was not conventionally hinged; rather, its front edge pivoted on a semi-circular channel moulded into the front of the engine bay, and was kept closed by a pair of clips on the front bulkhead. At the rear the boot lid was sunk into the rear deck, and sat on a rubber seal attached to a raised lip inside the opening, and there was a pair of drain holes in the opening, connected to the underside of the bodyshell by tubing.

Separate round rear lights comprised a red rear/stop light and amber indicator on each side. Foam-filled glass fibre bumpers were fitted front and rear, and masked the join between the two body mouldings. At the front sat the Elan's signature feature – pop-up headlamps – which when down gave the nose a clean and aerodynamic look. The lights were vacuum operated using a take-off from the inlet manifold, with the front crossmember of the chassis acting as a vacuum reservoir. When the lights were operated via a push/pull vacuum switch on the dash, a pair of operating pods with rubber diaphragms lifted up the hinged bowls to expose the headlights.

Until the later Series 4 cars the pop-ups operated in a 'fail-unsafe' mode – if the vacuum failed the pods went down and stayed down, which was not ideal.

The hood on the Series 1 and 2 cars was a 'build it yourself' affair, and had to be dismantled or raised manually, with the hood material separate from the steel hood frame. When not in use the hood and its stays could be stored in the boot.

The Elan's chassis or subframe was also very different to any other design. It was made from sheet steel, folded to form a rigid central box-shaped backbone, with a Y-shaped front end terminated by a crossmember carrying a pair of turrets at each end to provide the pickups for the

The interior of Paddy Byres' Elan S1. Note the delicate light alloy, wood-rimmed steering wheel, and how the wooden dashboard doesn't span the whole width of the cabin.

front suspension's twin wishbones. At the rear a second crossmember supported the differential and the top mounts for the rear suspension's Chapman struts, while a wide-based A frame was located on the lower edge of the backbone, the outer end of which carried the rear hub. The bodyshell was largely unstressed, although the wooden dashboard added rigidity to the overall structure. The bodyshell was bolted to the chassis and was characterised by the deep 'transmission tunnel' between the driver and passenger; essential to allow the body to sit over the box section backbone of the chassis.

The wheels were unique to Lotus. Initially the Elan had bolt-on wheels, but these were quickly replaced with knock-on quick release items, fixed in place with a screw-on central three-eared spinner, and driven by a set of pegs on the hub that engaged with holes in the wheel. The wheels were 4.5in wide, and initially took 145-13 tyres, although later cars had wider 155x13 tyres on the 4.5J wheels.

The Elan S2 was introduced in November 1964 after about 850 Series 1 cars had been produced. There were minimal changes – the foot pedals were reduced in size, the dashboard was made full width, the front brake callipers had larger pistons, the brake master cylinder was changed and, after about 100 or so S2s were produced, the rear lights were changed to integrated units sourced from Vauxhall.

The Elan S1 has rounded wheelarches. The wheels on this example are aftermarket 'Minilite' alloys; the S1 was originally fitted with bolt-on steel wheels.

The Elan S1 and S2 boot lid fitted flush on the top of the rear deck. This was changed for the S3 when the rear of the boot lid was extended to the back panel. Note also the round rear lights: a defining feature of the S1 and S2 Elans.

The S2 Elan was similar in appearance to the S1. This nice example owned by Brian Goodison has the original steel bolt-on wheels, and shows the neat foam-filled grp front bumper.

An S/E specification car with a lightly tuned engine was introduced in 1966, with a 115bhp version of the Twin Cam, a higher final drive, and a better specced interior, with inertia reel seatbelts, and carpet replacing the floor mats.

Elan S1 and S2 specification

ENGINE: Lotus Twin Cam, cast iron block, light alloy cylinder head, four-cylinder in-line, chain-driven double overhead camshaft. **Bore and stroke:** 82.55 x 72.75mm; **capacity:** 1558cc; **power:** 105bhp in standard form, 115bhp in S/E specification. Twin Weber DCOE carburettors.
GEARBOX: Ford four-speed plus reverse.
SUSPENSION: Front: Independent by upper and lower wishbones, coil springs, anti-roll bar; **rear:** Independent by wide spread lower wishbone and Chapman strut, coil springs.
STEERING: Rack and pinion.
BRAKES: Discs all round. **Front:** 9.5in (24.1cm); **rear:** 10in (24.5cm).
WHEELS AND TYRES: Pressed steel, 13in diameter 5.5J. Originally bolt-on, later peg-drive knock-on type. 145x13 tyres.
DIMENSIONS: Length: 145in (368.3cm); **width:** 56in (142.2cm); **track:** Front and rear: 47.5in (120.6cm); **height:** 41in (104.1cm); **wheelbase:** 84in (213.3cm).
WEIGHT: 1410lb (639.5kg).
PERFORMANCE: Top speed: 108mph (173.8kph), **0-60mph:** 9 seconds.

Lotus Type 36 (Elan coupé) and Type 45 – Series 3 and 4 (1965 to 1972)

The first and only major change to the Elan's bodyshell came with the first fixed head coupé (FHC) version of the car, the Lotus Type 36, introduced in 1965. The changes were also reflected in the open-topped Series 3 and 4 models. The revised bodyshell had squared-off rear wheelarches, and the boot lid was extended so its edge overlapped the end of the body, negating the need for the internal drains seen on the Series 1 and 2 cars.

The Elan SS was introduced during S3 production and incorporated various safety features, including recessed instruments and flush fitting rocker switches for the US market. This is Jeff Boughton's 1968 example, and features the Vauxhall sourced oval rear light units.

The one-piece oval rear lights from the Vauxhall parts bin replaced the separate lamps used on the Series 1 and early 2 cars. The coupé also introduced chromed frames for the door windows, which were now electrically operated. The coupé was intended to produce a more refined car that would cater for the class of sports car drivers who did not want an open car. The first examples of the coupé were simply an Elan with a roof, and had no real ventilation system – something the original Elan had no need of!

Owners were expected to get stale air out of the car by opening the electric windows. However, companies such as Ford were producing cars with passive airflow systems, and the coupé swiftly gained some aerodynamically designed vents on the C pillar, which allowed stale air to be extracted automatically as the car was in motion, and

With the S4 the Elan came of age. By now it was a well sorted, great handling sports car and was even fairly reliable. This is John Humfryes' 1969 S4.

The profile view of the S4 shows the new rear wheelarches with their squared-off tops.

made the car a lot easier to use, especially in damp conditions. The Elan SS, or Super Safety version, was introduced in November 1967, and incorporated minor modifications to the dashboard, interior and exterior to comply with new US safety legislation. With the introduction of the Series 4 cars (both Type 36 and Type 45) in 1968, the cars gained new larger rear light clusters, the base of which was shared with later E-Type Jaguars, but with Lotus' own configuration of the actual light elements.

The Type 45 was the convertible version of the Type 36, also made in Series 3 and Series 4 versions. With the Type 45 the body adopted the changes seen on the Type 36, and it had an all-new hood.

The new hood frame was bolted to the body, and the fabric was fixed to the frame. This meant that the frame and hood were effectively one piece, making it easy to to put up and down, with the assembly sitting in a well behind the cabin when lowered. Both the Type 36 and Type 45 Elans had electrically operated windows.

The final iteration of the Elan was the

A nice Series 4 Elan pictured at Castle Combe. Behind is the Elan's stablemate, a Lotus Europa Twin Cam.

Dave Groves' 1972 Sprint shows off the rear lights that were shared with the Plus 2.

Sprint, available in open and closed forms. The Sprint was introduced in October 1971 to give the Elan's sales a boost, and its modified Twin Cam engine had larger valves and hotter cams to give a claimed power output of 125bhp.

The Sprint's 'trade mark' was a two-tone paint job with white undersides and the normal body colour on top, separated by a gold coachline. However, a single colour was available as an optional extra. From October 1972 a few of the very last Sprints were also offered with Lotus' own five-speed gearbox, with the model called the Sprint/5. The Elan would remain in production until August 1973, when the introduction of VAT killed off the kit car market, which, along with the age of the car, meant that the Elan's time was up.

Elan S4 Sprint specification

ENGINE: Lotus Twin Cam, cast iron block, light alloy cylinder head, four-cylinder in-line, chain-driven double overhead camshaft. **Bore and stroke:** 82.55 x 72.75mm; **capacity:** 1558cc; **power:** (Sprint Spec) 125bhp. Twin Weber DCOE carburettors or Twin Stromberg 175 CD.
GEARBOX: Ford four-speed plus reverse.
SUSPENSION: Front: Independent by upper and lower wishbones, coil springs, anti-roll bar. **Rear:** Independent by wide spread lower wishbone and Chapman strut, coil springs.
STEERING: Rack and pinion.
BRAKES: Discs all round. **Front:** 9.5in (24.1cm); **rear:** 10in (24.5cm).
WHEELS AND TYRES: Pressed steel, 13in diameter, 5.5J peg-drive, knock-on type. 145x13 tyres.
DIMENSIONS: Length: 145in (368.3cm); **width:** 56in (142.2cm); **track front and rear:** 47.5in (120.6cm); **height:** 41in (104.1cm); **wheelbase:** 84in (213.3cm).
WEIGHT: 1590lb (721kg).
PERFORMANCE: Top speed: 120mph (193kph); **0-60 mph:** 7.0 seconds.

The Sprint came in open or coupé form. This is Dave Groves' 1972 Sprint in classic Lotus two-tone Sprint livery of Pistachio Green over white. Dave always fits classic Minilite alloys to his cars – these use the existing Lotus knock-on hubs and spinners.

Pictured at Castle Combe in 2013, this is an Elan Sprint in classic Lotus Yellow over white, next to a Europa also sporting a non-standard Sprint style paint job.

The engine bay of Dave Grove's Elan Sprint shows the car's twin Webers and the black crackle finished 'Big Valve' cam cover.

Dave Groves' 1972 Sprint coupé showing the air vents to the rear of the door that extract stale air from the interior.

The Lotus Type 50 The Plus 2 (1967 to 1974)

Notwithstanding the introduction of the Elan coupé Type 36, Chapman had realised that the more upmarket a car became the more it would sell for.

The 2+2 market was tempting – if a young and impetuous single bloke bought an Elan in his twenties, then why not give him the opportunity to buy a 2+2 to accommodate his wife and two children, and still satisfy his need for a sports car in his thirties? The result of this thinking appeared in the late 1960s with the Lotus Elan Plus 2. This was a stretched and widened Elan, sharing the well proven Elan mechanical underpinnings with a new chassis giving a longer wheelbase of 96in (243.8cm) compared to the Elan's 84in (213.3cm), which allowed for a longer cabin with two small seats behind the driver and passenger. The width was increased to 66.25in (168.2cm) compared to the Elan's 56in (142.2cm), which gave the passengers a bit more elbow room! However the new model's most striking feature was the totally restyled body.

With a passing resemblance to the Rover-BRM Gas Turbine car seen at Le Mans in 1963 and then again in 1965, the Elan Plus 2 was a two-door fixed head coupé with a striking flat front with pop-up headlamps and a sleek rear end with a fashionably flat cut-off tail. Very modern and aerodynamic, the Plus 2 was a luxury coupé that had almost the same level of performance as the Elan, but with a very

The blue Plus 2S and the red over white Sprint shows the increased width and overall size of the Plus 2.

upmarket level of trim and equipment, and a price to match. Selling at some £500 (about 33%) more than the Elan in 1967, the Plus 2, while using a small amount of extra materials and just a little more labour to build meant a move upmarket for Lotus. The adverts for the car emphasised the upmarket aspirations and price – in 1968 in the UK the Plus 2's price was a hefty £2197.

The interior reflected the sophisticated

This is the 60th Plus 2 to be made and it first hit the road in 1967. Owned by Melody and Henry Koslowski, the car is a very early survivor of the breed.

mechanicals and exterior styling, with an emphasis on the sporty but luxurious, with comfortable fully adjustable seats, a walnut veneered dashboard, full complement of Smiths round-faced instruments (speedo and tachometer, water temperature, fuel level, ammeter and oil pressure), many toggle switches to operate the minor functions, along with all mod cons, such as two-speed wipers, air-bleed heating, through-flow ventilation, two-speed fan and electric windows. That may sound like a poverty spec model today, but in the mid 1960s this was almost space age specification! The Plus 2 was a success, and was swiftly supplemented by the Plus 2S in

The rear end of Plus 2 number 60 shows the early rear lights that were shared with the then current Alfa Romeo 1600 coupé.

The inside of the early Plus 2 is a step up from the Elan, with a well stocked wooden dash and vinyl trim. This is the Koslowski's car no 60.

1969, which upped the luxury specification with a plusher interior and added a unique feature to the Plus 2 design with the adoption of new Smiths instruments featuring flat chrome bezels, dark grey faces, white lettering and DayGlo red needles.

As if the four minor instruments seen in the Plus 2 were not enough, the Plus 2S added an additional pair (ambient temperature and a clock) along with a fine smattering of extra warning lights and nine safety-oriented recessed rocker switches on the veneered dashboard to control minor operations.

The dash was featured in an advert for a famous brand of cigarette, with an airline pilot's uniformed arm (with the four gold braids of a Captain) reaching for the ashtray on the dash, all the while implying that the driver was in control.

Under the bonnet of the Plus 2 there are no surprises to Elan owners, but a lot more room. The Twin Cam engine with early 'Lotus' cam cover sports a pair of twin-choke Weber carburettors.

With minimal badging and sleek lines the Plus 2 was an attractive and fast little coupé. The car's steel front bumper came from the Ford Anglia 105E, and the car came as standard with Lotus steel knock-on wheels.

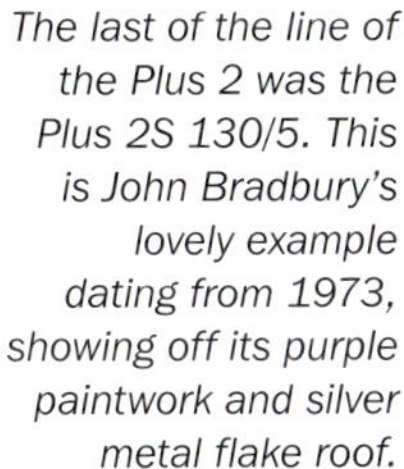

The last of the line of the Plus 2 was the Plus 2S 130/5. This is John Bradbury's lovely example dating from 1973, showing off its purple paintwork and silver metal flake roof.

With the headlights up the Plus 2 loses some of its sleek looks. Note the standard Lotus alloy wheels on John Bradbury's Plus 2S 130/5 pictured here.

The standard steel knock-on wheels were 6.5in wide, and could be had with a chromed rim and black painted inners. Standard tyres were 165x13 radials.

In 1971 the Plus 2S 130 was introduced. The new model had the Sprint specification engine (hence the '130', which was a slightly inflated reference to the engine power) and also came with the option of a silver metal flake finished roof. Initially this was intended to be formed in the gel coat, thus saving paint and effort, but the process was not always successful. There are examples of factory-produced single-colour cars with the metal flake finish under the clear gel coat, and other cars with the metal flake finish painted over the original gel coat. Either way, the two-tone finish gave the car a unique, flamboyant and very classy look, very much in tune with the customising trends of the time.

The other change was the fitment of ten-spoke light alloy wheels, the rim and outer edges of the spokes finished in natural alloy, with black-painted inserts. These new wheels retained the peg drive seen with the steel wheels and were fitted with either three-eared or, for safety, octagonal chromed spinners. The looks got even classier in 1973 with the

The last of the Plus 2s had an even more plush interior than the first models. This is John Bradbury's Plus 2S 130/5 dash, with oatmeal trim and a five-speed gearbox.

From the rear, the styling of the last Plus 2s was very similar to the first models. Many of the later models had the roof finished in metal flake, giving the cars a very 1970s vibe.

production of a limited edition JPS black and gold version commemorating the marque winning the Formula 1 championship in 1972. The mechanical elements remained much the same until the introduction of the Sprint specification engine in 1972, resulting in the designation Plus 2S 130, and then, in 1972, the option to have the new Lotus five-speed gearbox resulting in the Plus 2S 130/5. Production of the Plus 2 ended in 1974.

Elan Plus 2 specification

ENGINE: Lotus Twin Cam, cast iron block, light alloy cylinder head, four-cylinder in-line, chain-driven double overhead camshaft. **Bore and stroke:** 82.55 x 72.75mm; **capacity:** 1558cc. Twin Weber DCOE carburettors or twin Stromberg 175 CD.
GEARBOX: Ford four-speed plus reverse.
SUSPENSION: Front: Independent by upper and lower wishbones, coil springs, anti-roll bar; **rear:** Independent by wide spread lower wishbone and Chapman strut, coil springs.
STEERING: Rack and pinion.
BRAKES: Discs all round. **Front:** 9.5in (24.1cm); **rear:** 10in (24.5cm).
WHEELS AND TYRES: Pressed Steel, 13in diameter 5.5J peg-drive knock-on type. 145x13 tyres.
DIMENSIONS: Length: 169.75in (428.6cm); **width:** 66.25in (168.2cm); **track front:** 54in (137cm); **track rear:** 55in (139.7cm); **height:** 47in (119.3cm); **wheelbase:** 96in (243.8cm).
WEIGHT: 2086lb (946kg).
PERFORMANCE: Top speed: 118mph (190kph); **0-60mph:** 9.0 seconds.

John Bradbury's 1973 Plus 2S 130/5 out for a run in the rain.

MID-ENGINED MARVEL: THE LOTUS EUROPA

The Lotus Europa was initially designed as a cheap and cheerful replacement for the hardcore motorsports-oriented Lotus Seven, slotting into the range below the contemporary Lotus Elan. However, when the car eventually hit the market in December 1966, it was a very different animal. The new car was a small but sophisticated GT, with a fully trimmed interior and a mid-mounted engine. The car was aimed at the European market in the first instance, and was available only in left-hand drive. Its mainstream Renault engine and gearbox meant that there was plenty of mechanical expertise on the Continent available to sort out any problems.

The Europa could not have come about without a collaboration between Lotus and Renault. The early Europas used the engine and transaxle from the Renault 16, which, although front-engined and front-wheel drive, importantly had its engine mounted behind the gearbox, and tucked-in under the bonnet close to the bulkhead. For the Europa the whole engine and transaxle assembly from the Renault 16 was turned through 180 degrees, so that the engine was ahead of the transaxle. The one problem with this switch was that the Europa would, as things stood, have four reverse gears and only one forward gear ... not ideal! Renault switched the main drive gear of the differential around – a relatively easy engineering job – which reversed the final drive direction and gave the Europa a mid-mounted engine with its gearbox behind, as well as the ideal weight distribution, as seen on the latest racing cars. The existence of the Renault powertrain was essential for the Europa. Having sourced the major mechanical elements of the car, Lotus was then able to craft a superb little GT with room for two people and just enough luggage space to fulfil its brief.

Martin Ricketts' Series 1 Europa shows the clean lines of the front end. Note the only indicator is the small orange side lamp behind the headlamp. The front bumper is from the 105E Anglia and shared with the Plus 2.

The rear three-quarter view shows the rear buttresses that were such an important styling feature, although they constrained rear quarter vision.

There was a small luggage compartment behind the engine in the Europa. Luggage in it was prone to getting warm!

The Renault power unit was a snug fit in the Europa Series 1 engine bay. However, there was adequate space around it for routine maintenance.

The Europa became more mainstream with the Series 2, which solved most of the faults exhibited by the Series 1, and was made available to home and export markets. The final iterations of the Europa were the Europa Twin Cam and Special models. These saw the Renault engine replaced with Lotus' home-grown Twin Cam unit, and were in production until the mid 1970s.

Europa Series 1 – Type 46 (1966 to 1968)

The Renault engine used in the Europa was a sophisticated little unit. In line with Lotus' philosophy of using small capacity but relatively high power engines it displaced a mere 1470cc from a bore and stroke of 76 x 81mm, but produced a healthy 78bhp at 6000rpm and 76lb/ft of torque at 4000rpm, and weighed a svelte 200lb. The engine had an alloy crankcase and cylinder head, steel wet liners, and the crankshaft was supported on five main bearings, giving the bottom end tremendous strength. The camshaft was mounted high on the side of the engine in an oil filled trough, and the eight valves were operated by short pushrods that helped the engine to rev freely.

The combustion chamber was wedge shaped, with the valves angled at 20 degrees to the engine centre line, promoting good swirl and efficient combustion. The unit used in the Europa had a new camshaft, larger inlet valves and a higher compression ratio of 10.25:1 when compared with the standard Renault 16 unit.

All Series 1 cars were left-hand drive, and aimed at the European market. The cabin was small and sparse but neatly laid out and fitted with all the essentials.

Bolted directly to the end of the engine, the four-speed and reverse transmission was similarly encased in a lightweight all alloy casting, making for a light and compact engine transmission unit. The integral differential in the transmission casing had its drive wheel reversed, and the final drive to the rear wheels was by solid driveshafts with Hookes universal joints at each end.

The Europa chassis built on the experience gained on producing the Elan. Like the Elan the Europa chassis was a 'Y' shaped backbone

The Europa Series 2 came to the market in April 1968; this is John Rand's 1969 example. Now available in right-hand drive, the Series 2's bodyshell was bolted to the car's chassis, making crash repairs a lot easier.

affair, but reversed, with the two ends of the 'Y' at the back to cradle the engine, and pick up the rear suspension elements. At the front there was a simple box section crosspiece that had pickups for the front suspension and steering rack. The front suspension was very similar to that of the Elan, with twin unequal length wishbones supporting Alford and Alder uprights as seen on the Triumph Herald, and carried a disc brake on the hub. An anti-roll bar was connected to the bottom wishbone, and used a long drop link from the top front wishbone's pivot bolt to locate it.

At the rear there was a long, fabricated steel box section trailing radius arm that connected the bottom of the hub carrier to the chassis, and a transverse link rod that ran from the centreline of the chassis to the bottom of the hub. Finally, there was a Chapman strut – a combined spring and shock absorber – connecting the hub to the top of the chassis. The rear brakes were conventional 8in (20.3cm) drums mounted on the rear hubs.

The body followed the practice established with the Elan, and was made from glass fibre mouldings. The car had a low-slung front end, but, rather than pop-up headlamps, as used on the Elan for simplicity, the headlamps were fixed and integrated into the front of the front wings. The front luggage compartment also formed the plenum chamber for the integrated ventilation system, which was pressurised by air entering from the front grille. There were three ducts feeding air from this chamber into the cabin – one on each side connected to Renault adjustable vents at each end of the dash. These ducts fed fresh air into the cabin, while a central vent fed air into the heater box where it was warmed and distributed to the cabin and

The S2 Europa retained the lines of the S1. This is John Rand's example, seen here in the Surrey hills. Note the Cosmic alloy wheels that replaced the steel wheels seen on the S1.

The rear end of the Europa S2 now shared its rear lights with the S4 Elan and later Plus 2. The narrow rear window and high rear buttresses are apparent in this shot.

With the S2 the Europa gained a pair of round indicators mounted on the nose above the Ford Anglia front bumper.

windscreen with fan assistance. Stale air was extracted from the cabin via slots in the roof, just behind the top of the rear window.

Initially, the side windows were fixed in place because the integrated airflow system was thought to provide adequate ventilation. In reality, however, it didn't work very well, so the windows were modified fairly early on to make the whole pane removable. The door cards were modified at the same time to provide a slot to store the removed glass. Issues with the ventilation system were that it did not work too well when the car was moving slowly, and in traffic the low position of the front grille meant that traffic fumes were sucked into the cabin. The chamber also contained the spare wheel, while the right-hand side front wheelarch housed the air exit for the engine cooling radiator.

Pictured at Castle Combe in 2018 this is a lovely yellow example of Series 2 Europa. A pair of M100 Elans are in the background.

With a new engine came some styling changes. The Europa Twin Cam's rear buttresses were cut down and the wheelbase extended slightly. This is Royston Bing's lovely example.

The cabin featured built in mouldings for the fixed position seats, and the pedal box position could be moved backwards or forwards to accommodate occupants of various sizes. The instrument panel was a simple, natural finish alloy plate, positioned in front of the driver, and carrying the speedometer and tachometer. The centre console was similarly covered in an alloy sheet, and had the four minor instruments (water temperature, oil pressure, fuel gauge and ammeter) in a line at the top, and the minor switches lower down above the ashtray. The choke and heater controls were placed on the central tunnel behind the gear lever, and had to be pulled forwards to operate them. The handbrake was a pull-on umbrella handle-type, mounted under the dash.

At the rear of the cabin a small slot of a window gave some view of what was behind, across the top of the engine compartment lid. However, a pair of 'flying buttresses', one on each side of the car above the level of the engine compartment lid, restricted the rear quarter view, creating two massive blind spots for the driver. A large single windscreen wiper swept the screen.

There were no conventional door handles, simply a push-button lock on the door and a recess moulded into the body behind the door so you could press the button with you thumb and pull open the door with your fingers. This was a neat and typically Chapman solution to simplifying a design and reducing the number of components used. The engine compartment lid was originally fixed in place by slotting its front under a lip below the rear screen, and it was fixed in place with a pair of clips on the trailing edge. Later Series 1 models were fitted with a more conventional system: a pair of hinges at the front but retaining the locking clips. On each side of the lid was a pair of grilles, with a further grille running across the width of the car on the horizontal rear panel between the Lancia-supplied tail light clusters. The purpose of these grilles was to cool the engine compartment. Taking advantage of a low pressure area at the rear of the car, hot air was extracted from the engine compartment via the rear grille, with new cold air entering the compartment from the top ones.

The first generation Series 1 Europa did have issues, including the inefficient ventilation system described above, but more important was the cost and difficulty in repairing accident damage. While the chassis was a simple backbone unit like on the Elans, it was bonded onto the glass fibre body. If the car was involved in an accident that damaged the chassis, this could result in a very expensive repair bill, especially if the repairer did not understand that it was possible to remove the old chassis and bond in a new one.

The original Series 1 model was only available in left-hand drive, and was aimed at the Continental market – hence the name (some contemporary Lotus literature refers to the car as the 'Europe'). However there was considerable interest in the car from the domestic market, and Lotus quickly introduced

Painted in Lotus Yellow, the Europa Twin Cam basks in the sun at a Club Lotus meet. Fitted with aftermarket but period Wolfrace slot alloys, this is a fine example.

a new version, the Series 2. Having learned from the experience of building and testing the Series 1, Lotus produced a much more practical car in the Series 2 during 1968.

Lotus Type 54 and 65, Europa Series 2 (1968 to 1971)

Most of the problems of the S1 were addressed with the introduction of the Series 2 model in August 1968. Retaining the Renault engine and transmission of the Series 1, the Series 2 was made available in right-hand drive for the home market as well as left-hand drive for the European and US markets. Importantly, to assuage the fears of the insurance and repair companies, it had its chassis bolted to the body, making it a lot easier to repair accident damage. The ventilation system was improved, with conventional electrically operated side windows giving the occupants much more control over the cabin environment. To fit the electric windows the cars gained a small triangular quarter light at the front of the door; oddly this was fixed in place, and the chance to fit opening quarter-lights and the attendant ventilation benefits they would have brought were lost. The seats were conventional, and were now mounted on the floor on sliders giving some fore and aft adjustment and allowing the pedal box to be fixed in place. The cabin remained cramped, though, and the small doors still restricted ease of access.

The twin cam-powered Europa benefited from improved visibility thanks to the removal of the rear buttresses. However, the rear window was still tiny, as can be seen in this shot.

Despite the downfalls of the Series 1 cars, with the introduction of the Series 2 most of the issues were solved. The famous English journalist Denis Jenkinson took a Series 2 Europa for a trans-European tour in 1969, travelling some 3645 miles (5871km) in 14 days, from his home in Hampshire all the way to Sicily to cover that year's Targa Florio, and he came back with the

Royston Bing's Twin Cam Special Europa is a 1974 model, and is immaculate. This shot shows the Lotus alloy wheels and the cut down rear buttresses.

opinion that the Europa was a fine GT car, admirably suited to covering large distances economically and quickly.

To restore performance after the introduction of ever more onerous emissions controls in May 1969 Lotus introduced the left-hand drive only Type 65 Europa. Not only did this model incorporate the numerous changes needed to meet the ever more strict US safety and emissions regulations, it also got a larger version of the Renault engine to try to maintain the car's performance. The engine was the Renault A2L 1565cc engine, the increased displacement achieved by increasing the bore by 1mm and the stroke by 3mm (to 77 x 84mm, respectively). In this state the engine produced 80bhp at 6000rpm and had torque of 79lb/ft at 4000rpm. This restored the car's performance to original levels and met the legislation to enable the car to be sold in the USA.

While the Series 2 Europa was available in right-hand drive for the home market and addressed the two major problems found with the Series 1, namely the ventilation system and the bonded-on chassis, it did not offer any real performance increase over the Series 1. The performance of the car's rivals had increased over the years, and the Europa was being left behind; it was viewed as an old design with some insurmountable issues – notably the poor rear three-quarter vision thanks to the 'flying buttresses'. It would take a redesign of the body and a new power plant to address these problems and take the Europa into the 1970s.

Europa Series 1 and 2 specification

ENGINE: Renault light alloy block and cylinder head, four-cylinder in-line, chain-driven single high mounted cam with pushrod-operated valves. **Bore and stroke:** 76 x 81mm; **capacity:** 1470cc. Single Solex 35 DIDSA twin-choke carburettor.
GEARBOX: Renault four-speed plus reverse.
SUSPENSION: Front: Independent by unequal length double wishbones with anti-roll bar. Coil spring over telescopic dampers; **rear:** Independent with long fabricated steel radius arm, fixed length drive shafts and tubular lateral link. Coil spring over telescopic dampers.
STEERING: Rack and pinion.
BRAKES: Front: 9.75in (24.76cm) discs; **rear:** 8in (20.32cm) drums.
WHEELS AND TYRES: Pressed steel, 13in diameter, 4.5J, steel, bolt-on. 155x13 tyres.
DIMENSIONS: Length: 157.25in (399.4cm); **width:** 64.5in (163.8cm); **track front and rear:** 53in (134.6cm); **height:** 42.5in (107.9cm); **wheelbase:** 91in (231.1cm).
WEIGHT: 1566lb (710.3kg).
PERFORMANCE: Top speed: 110mph (190kph); **0-60mph:** 9.5 seconds.

Lotus Type 74 – the Twin Cam Europa (1971 to 1974)

The final versions of the Europa were fitted with Lotus' own Twin Cam engine, which, as well as giving the cars a welcome performance boost, had a subtle restyle that made the cars a little more practical. It was a bit of a design struggle to squeeze the larger engine into the space; one of the design stipulations was that there would be only minimal changes to the chassis and body dimensions.

However, despite the increased length of the Lotus engine, compared to the original Renault unit, the engineering team, led by Mike Kimberley, managed to achieve it with only a small increase in the wheelbase (now 91.7in (233.7cm) compared to the original Renault-engined car's 91in (231.14cm). This meant that no changes to the bottom half of the bodyshell were required. The new car retained the Renault trans axle.

The major change to be made to the bodyshell was to cut down the 'Flying Buttresses'. While this did little to address the overall poor rear visibility, it did mean that the driver had a slightly less restricted rear three-quarter view out of the letterbox-sized rear window.

The Lotus Twin Cam engine in the Europa initially produced a relatively healthy 105bhp at 6000rpm along with 108lb/ft of torque at 5000rpm compared to S2's 78bhp and 74lb/ft. Later versions of the Twin Cam car received the Sprint specification big-valve motor that gave 126bhp at 6500rpm and 113ft/lb of torque at 4500rpm. While the weight of the car increased to 1578lb (721kg) compared to the Series 2's 1566lb (710kg), the car's performance with the 105bhp motor went up significantly, with a top speed of 118mph and a 0-60 time of some 7.0 seconds, compared to the S2's 110mph and 0-60 in 10.7 seconds.

The Europa Twin Cam Special still has a reasonably sized front luggage compartment. The spare wheel is stored in the car's nose.

The Lotus twin cam engine was a tight fit in the engine bay, as can be seen in this shot of Royston Bing's Special. By the time Royston's car was built Lotus had switched from Weber to Dellorto twin-choke carburettors.

This was sufficient to revitalise the car and sales were good in both home and export markets. The Twin Cam engine was especially popular in the USA. Other changes made were to increase the space around the pedals and fit a bigger fuel tank with 12 gallon (54-litre) capacity, the utility of which was offset somewhat by the car's increased fuel consumption.

Other than the removal of the buttresses and the new engine, the Twin Cam Europa remained much the same as the Series 2, with few other updates. However, the biggest change came with the introduction of the Twin Cam Special model that, with its 125bhp pushed the top speed up to an impressive 121mph (196kph) and pushed the 0-60 time down to 6.6 seconds.

The last Twin Cam came off the line in 1974, whereupon mid-engine enthusiasts would have to wait until 1976 to own a new

The Twin Cam Special's interior was nicely fitted out, with a wooden full-width dash and a neat centre console. It was much more luxurious than the S1 and S2 cars.

mid-engined Lotus, when the all-new Lotus Esprit broke cover.

There was one more variant of the Europa: the Europa GS. This was not actually a Lotus model but was produced by GS Cars of Warmley to update the Europa. Using new glass fibre panels, bonded to the original body, the GS was designed by William Towns and Mike Rawlings in the classic 1970s wedge style with pop-up headlights and a pair of 'flying buttresses' running each side of the engine bay. The new body panels covered wider wheels, and the car was in many ways a successful update of the Europa. However, by the time the kit was on the market the Esprit had also arrived, which made the GS redundant.

Europa Twin Cam specification

ENGINE: Lotus Twin Cam, cast iron block, light alloy cylinder head, four-cylinder in-line, chain-driven double overhead camshaft. **Bore and stroke:** 82.55 x 72.75mm; **capacity:** 1558cc. Twin Weber DCOE carburettors or Twin Stromberg 175 CD.
GEARBOX: Renault four-speed plus reverse.
SUSPENSION: Front: Independent by unequal length double wishbones with anti-roll bar. Coil spring over telescopic dampers. **Rear:**

Royston Bing's Twin Cam Europa is a lovely looking car. Note the sill trims that help to make the car look slimmer.

The rear three-quarter view of Royston Bing's Twin Cam Special shows the bolt-on alloy wheels and the rear end. The rear bumper was a Mark 2 Cortina item.

The Europa GS was not a Lotus model, but a glass fibre body kit to update the Europa's style. Produced in the 1970s these cars had flying buttresses and a wedge shape with pop-up headlamps.

The Twin Cam Europa with an Esprit – the car that would replace the Europa in the Lotus range.

Independent with long fabricated steel radius arm, fixed-length drive shafts and tubular lateral link. Coil spring over telescopic dampers.
STEERING: Rack and pinion.
BRAKES: Front: 9.75in (24.76cm) diameter discs; **rear:** 8in (20.32cm) diameter drums.
WHEELS AND TYRES: Pressed steel, 13in diameter, 4.5J, steel, bolt-on. 155x13 tyres.
DIMENSIONS: Length: 157.25in (399.4cm); **width:** 64.5in (163.8cm); **track front and rear:** 53in (134.6cm); **height:** 42.5in (107.9cm); **wheelbase:** 91.7in (233.7cm).
WEIGHT: 1588lb (721kg).
PERFORMANCE: Top speed: 120mph (190kph), **0-60mph:** 8.2 seconds.

THE NEW GUARD – THE ELITE, ÉCLAT, AND EXCEL

The advent of the new Elite in 1974 marked Lotus' move upmarket, and also reflected Chapman's age and family responsibilities. With the Elan, the market was the young single enthusiast, the Plus 2 delivered a car aimed at the enthusiast with a young family, and the Elite was aimed at the enthusiast who had matured into a successful businessman, with grown-up children and a need to transport business associates in some comfort. The new Elite was designed to accommodate four adults in some luxury, but also provide Lotus levels of performance and roadholding.

Sitting alongside the Elite was a cheaper coupé version, the Éclat, and then the mid-engined Esprit arrived in 1976 to give Lotus a proper sports car to head its range. The Elite suffered from poor sales, and it was its coupé brother, the Éclat that was developed into the sophisticated, reliable and good looking Excel that won the day. The Esprit went from strength to strength, with the Turbo versions giving the car the performance to match its looks, and finally, with a new softer shape and a new V8 engine, the Esprit became a proper British-made supercar.

In 1989, and produced alongside the Esprit, came the M100 Elan, a short-lived project to produce a small sports car. It was not a success, alas, mainly due to its front-wheel drive platform.

The Lotus Type 75 and 83 Elite (1974 to 1982)

By the early 1970s Lotus had identified where it wanted to go – in step with the increasing age of its existing customers Lotus thought the way ahead was a true four-seater Grand Tourer, which led to the Type 75 Elite, introduced in 1974. It made sense – Lotus' customer base bought the Elan in the 1960s, then, as families and a desire for more sophistication came along, the Plus 2 provided the answer. The Elan Sprint along with the Europa Twin Cam delivered high performance sports cars, but the Plus 2S was faltering – a larger high-performance four-seater was needed.

Engine-wise, Lotus had a new unit – the 900 series engine was an all-new, two-litre, four-cylinder DOHC all-alloy unit with state-of-the-art four valves per cylinder and the potential to have its capacity increased to 2.2 litres. It was designed to form the basis for a V8 version, which, unfortunately, never materialised. The engine was a four-cylinder unit with its bores slanted over at 45 degrees to the vertical to keep the engine height low and to facilitate the stillborn V8

The Lotus Elite of 1974 was a logical step for Lotus, and moved the company upmarket where margins were greater, increasing the chance of making a profit. The Elite was a three-door, four-seater designed for the successful executive who wanted Lotus levels of performance and handling.

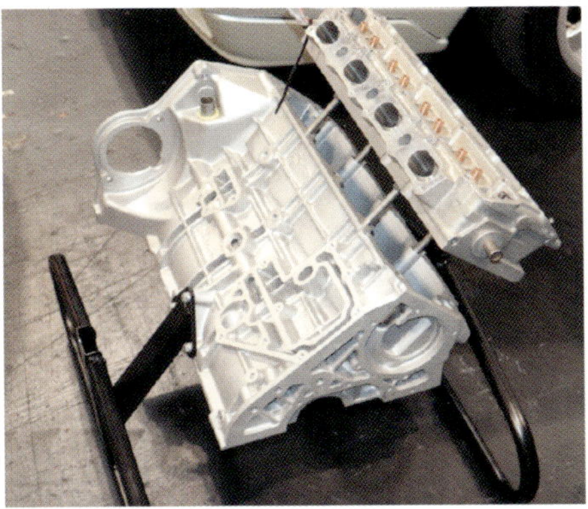

The Elite, Éclat and Excel were powered by Lotus' new 2-litre engine. Here is a bare block and head, showing the all-alloy construction and extensive strengthening ribs on the main casting.

This is a 2.2-litre engine, fitted to Leigh Greenham's Series 2.2 Elite from 1980 – one of the last ones made.

version. While the engine is often described as being developed from the similar-sized Vauxhall slant four this is incorrect. The only connection between the two units is that the iron-blocked Vauxhall unit has almost identical bore centres and shared the bore and stroke. These common characteristics meant that a few Vauxhall blocks were used to help develop the Lotus four-valve-per-cylinder head design, and a few engines, designated LV220 and LV240, were produced that used the Vauxhall blocks and Lotus heads in the Lotus 62 Group 6 prototype racer of 1969. However, even a quick glance at the 900 series engine shows fundamental differences from the Vauxhall engine, with the latter's conventional cast iron block and separate main bearing caps. The Lotus unit has an all alloy crankcase comprised of three castings making up three 'layers' – in effect a sandwich made up of the cylinder block, main bearing carrier, and sump.

The top layer was the cylinder block itself,

This 1976 Elite pictured at Castle Combe in 2013 shows the unique Lotus alloy wheels and the stainless steel trim surrounding the windows. Also visible is the rubbing strip used to conceal the join between the two body mouldings.

The front end of this 1976 Elite shows the pronounced 'wedge' style of the car. The pop-up headlamps made this styling possible.

incorporating the bores, the steel liners, and the top half of the main bearing carriers. Below this sat a full-width, one-piece alloy casting which comprised the five bottom caps of the main bearings and the lower crankcase sides. Each of the main bearing caps were attached to the upper crankcase by two bolts. The bottom casting was the alloy sump, and this and the middle casting were fixed to the top casting by shared bolts positioned around the periphery of both castings. The design meant the engine had an immensely strong bottom end, and the unit happily took the increases in power that came with the 2.2-litre and turbocharged versions.

The engine was not the only innovation seen on the Elite. Having gained a great deal of experience with glass fibre manufacturing techniques, Lotus introduced a new system to semi-automate the production of the Elite bodyshells, rather than continue to use the hand lay-up methods seen on the Elan and Europa. The new Vacuum Assisted Resin Injection (VARI) system used air pressure to inject the resin into a two-piece mould that was pre-coated with the gel coat and had pre-cut glass fibre matting already in position. The bodyshell of the Elite was made from two mouldings, one top, one bottom.

The production process for the body parts was as follows: the two halves of the mould had the gel coat painted on, and this was then left to go off. The pre-cut glass fibre mat was then laid on one half, and the two parts were then bolted together forming a single mould. The air was then pumped out, and the resin,

The profile of the Elite shows an elongated roof and rear end hatch. The styling was probably least successful on the rear quarter, which gave the car a slightly heavy look.

The Elite's rear hatch was simply the rear window in a thin frame. While similar in concept to the Reliant Scimitar GTE, the Elite's boot was separated from the passenger cabin by a window positioned just behind the rear seats.

with slow acting hardener added, was then sucked in through carefully selected points on the mould using atmospheric pressure.

The correct positioning of the injection points was vital to ensure complete and consistent filling of the mould with the resin. Once the resin had set, the moulds were unbolted and the complete body half was released.

The VARI process had several benefits: It eliminated the human error that could occur in hand lay-up; the glass fibre mat was pre-cut and positioned precisely in the mould; there was a uniform distribution of resin, eliminating voids and dry patches; and the resin/hardener mix was pre-prepared so was the same throughout the process and cured consistently across the moulding. Finally, each bodyshell half had gel coat on both sides, so there was no bare glass fibre matt exposed in the finished bodyshell. This meant that there was a waterproof barrier across the whole of the bodyshell, markedly reducing paint issues as there was no potential for the wicking or osmosis that caused the blistering and bubbling often seen on the earlier hand laid-up Elans and Europas.

The complete body was simply constructed by glueing the top and bottom halves together. A glued-on rubbing strip was then applied along the join, which not only served to conceal the join, it also protected the body at its widest point.

Having looked at the underlying technology it's time to look at the cars themselves. The first of the new models was the Elite, an odd backward reference to the original Type 14 Elite, as the new car was firmly aimed at Lotus' ageing customer base, as already mentioned. Engineering of the new car was headed up by Lotus chief Mike Kimberley, and the car's styling was created by designer Oliver Winterbottom. The car was a three-door hatchback with a low, wedge-shaped front and a cut-off rear. Access to the four-seat cabin was via the two conventional doors, while boot access was via a glass hatch, a similar design to that of the Reliant Scimitar GTE. Engineering-wise the car followed established Lotus practice of a folded sheet steel backbone chassis sitting under the glass fibre bodyshell. At the front end there was independent suspension and disc front brakes using hardware from the General Motors parts bin, along with Lotus' new 2-litre engine and the five-speed manual gearbox first seen in the Elan and Plus 2, or the option of a Borg Warner three-speed automatic. In the middle was the box section backbone, and at the rear there was independent suspension that used the drive shafts as the top links, with long trailing arms to control fore and aft location.

The rear brakes were positioned inboard to cut down unsprung weight but were drums rather than discs – presumably a cost-cutting measure. The bolt-on light alloy wheels were unique to Lotus design, with the aerodynamic design, that was basically obligatory at the time, to help vent the front disc brakes.

The Elite's interior was nicely styled and trimmed to a high standard. This is Leigh Greenham's S2.2 from 1980, which has a full leather interior.

The interior of the Elite reflected its upmarket aspirations. A well stocked dashboard, mounted in a binnacle ahead of the driver and featuring a full set of round black-bezelled Smiths instruments, provided all the necessary information, while minor switches, heating and ventilation controls, clock and the radio were mounted on the centre console, which had a good dose of fake wood facings. There was a non-reflective flock finish for the dash top instrument binnacle, and the seats were cloth-covered (with the option of leather). Driver and passenger seats featured manual adjustment in most directions, while the rear seating – strictly for two: the central tunnel making it impossible to accommodate a fifth passenger – were heavily sculptured and formed by the bodyshell moulding itself, with not a lot of padding. They did, however, accommodate normal sized adults in reasonable comfort, with plenty of headroom thanks to the hatchback configuration and the extended rear roofline of the bodyshell. Access to the rear seats was somewhat restricted by the two-door body configuration.

The doors were long, and fitted with a horizontal steel beam, positively located on the A and B pillars when the door was closed to provide side impact protection. The front seat mechanism allowed the seats to be moved forwards easily to facilitate access to the rear, without the need for too much contortion. One surprising aspect of the body design was that the passenger compartment was separated from the glass hatchback-accessed boot by a glass window just behind the rear seats. While this cut down noise and the possibility of exhaust or fuel fumes being drawn into the passenger compartment, it did negate a lot of the practicality of the three-door hatchback design.

A controversial aspect of the bodyshell was the rear styling. While the front end was sleek and purposeful, and from most aspects the car looked good, some thought the rear three-quarter view ungainly, heavy and lumpen, with a large expanse of body evident above and behind the rear wheels. Obviously this was needed to accommodate the hatchback rear end, and the high roof line was needed to give the rear passengers decent headroom, but it could have looked better – as evidenced by the Éclat's fastback styling.

The various safety features incorporated into the Elite's design led to it being awarded the prestigious Don Safety Trophy in 1975.

The Elite got a mid-life refresh in 1980, receiving the updated 2.2-litre Lotus engine and various cosmetic updates, including a neat front spoiler and a new rear bumper with integrated Rover SD1 rear lights. Although named the Elite Series 2.2, the update was initially called the Series 2. The cars also got new alloy wheels, the design of which was first seen on the 1978 Series 2 Esprit.

Poor sales figures meant that Elite

The rear three-quarter view of the Elite is probably its least attractive aspect. Note the Series 2 style rear bumper with its square number plate and Rover SD1 rear lights.

The best view of the Elite is from the front, with the wedge styling and large glass area giving the car a great appearance. This is Leigh Greenham's 1980 S2.2.

The rear end of the S2.2 shows the hatch and the Rover SD1 rear lights.

production eventually fizzled out in 1982, leaving just the Esprit and Éclat in the range.

All in all the Elite was a neat, practical and, to the author's eye at least, an appealing design. The car never really sold in the numbers Lotus expected – it was probably a bit too unconventional as a design. One suspects that most potential customers had grown out of the need for superlative roadholding and performance, and put their money into more prosaic offerings from Jaguar, Mercedes and BMW, with their equivalent performance, prestige and luxury, but also, probably most importantly, four doors.

Lotus Elite specification

ENGINE: Lotus 900 series all-alloy, four-cylinder, belt-driven DOHC 16-valve. **Bore and stroke:** 95.2 x 69.2mm; **capacity:** 1973cc; **power:** 155bhp at 6500rpm; **torque:** 135lb/ft at 5000rpm. Twin Dellorto twin-choke carburettors.
GEARBOX: Lotus five-speed manual.
SUSPENSION: Front: Independent with top wishbone and single lower link, single coil over damper, anti-roll bar. **Rear:** Independent, by transverse link, semi trailing arm, single coil over damper.
STEERING: Rack and pinion.
BRAKES: Front: 10.4in (26.4cm) diameter discs, opposed piston calliper; **rear:** 9in (22.8cm) diameter drums.
WHEELS AND TYRES: GKN Alloy 7Jx14, 205/60VR14.
DIMENSIONS: Length: 175.5in (445.7cm); **width:** 71.5in (181.6cm); **track:** 58.5in (148.6cm) front, 59in (150cm) rear; **height:** 47.5in (120.7cm); **wheelbase:** 97.8in (248.4cm).
WEIGHT: 2552lb (1157kg).
PERFORMANCE: Top speed: 124mph (201kph); **0-60:** 7.8 seconds.

The Type 76 and 84 Lotus Éclat (1975 to 1982)

Launched in 1975, a year after the new Elite, the Éclat was initially a cut-price version of the former, with lower equipment levels and, most noticeably, a restyled cut-down rear end housing a conventional boot rather than the Elite's innovative rear hatch. Initially marketed as a cheaper coupé version of the Elite, the Éclat actually proved to be a longer-lasting

Pictured at Castle Combe in 2013, here are three Elites in a row. The centre car is a Series 1, flanked by a pair of S2.2s.

The Éclat was introduced after the Elite, and was a coupé version with a conventional boot rather than the Elite's rear hatch. This early car shows off the air vents in the bonnet.

design, despite the new body shape robbing the rear seat passengers of headroom.

Initially the Éclat came with steel wheels and a four-speed Ford gearbox, and was cheaper than the Elite. However, thanks to customer demand, equipment levels, and the price, crept up to Elite levels over time, probably due to the more conventional styling of the Éclat being more appealing to the paying public.

In 1977 Lotus offered the Éclat Sprint in an attempt to attract more sporting drivers. This was a special edition version of the standard Éclat with the Elite's alloy wheels and the option of the five-speed gearbox and different axle ratios to boost performance and drivability. The Éclat was facelifted along with the Elite in 1980, creating Series 2 and Series 2.2 models – both of which had the 2.2-litre engine. Like the Elite facelift the Éclat benefited visually from a new front spoiler, larger rear bumper and Rover SD1 rear lights. The new engine gave the same power but had a welcome increase in torque making the car easier and more relaxing to drive.

Initially the Éclat Sprint was a cut price 'entry level' car. The low spec was compensated for by stripes and badging; this car has the Lotus alloy wheels rather than the standard steel wheels.

The Lotus Excel (1982 to 1992)

Although the Éclat started off as a cheaper, and less well-equipped coupé version of the Elite, the car managed to outlive its more upmarket forerunner, probably thanks to the more conventional styling. Initially presented to the world as the Éclat Excel, the Éclat name was dropped fairly rapidly and the car became simply the Lotus Excel.

The Excel came about when the Éclat was given a major revamp for 1982, with the objective of updating the looks and aerodynamics, and making the mechanical elements of the car better and more reliable. Thanks to Lotus' new relationship with Toyota, this meant the car got a Toyota gearbox (which was quieter and more reliable than the Maxi-based Lotus five-speed unit), Toyota ventilated front disc brakes, and new Toyota drive shafts and outboard disc brakes at the rear.

At the same time Lotus took the opportunity to revise the rear suspension, fitting new top links, which meant the drive shaft no longer had to act as a top link. Many other minor parts were replaced with Toyota-sourced items, including the door handles.

Externally, the aerodynamics were overhauled, with a new chin spoiler/front bumper, along with a neat low-profile wing on the boot lid, and subtle body kit side skirts joining the front and rear bumpers. The

The Éclat was updated with new Toyota gearbox and rear end to become the Éclat Excel, as seen here.

The Elite (to the right) can be compared to the later Excels seen here in 2014 at Brands Hatch.

The Excel was the last of the range that started with the Elite. This is Martin Bradbury's 1991 Excel SE. The pop-up headlights in their pods are a distinctive feature of the car.

The Excel's coupé styling lost a little rear headroom, but gave the car a nicely balanced look. This is Martin Bradbury's 1991 example.

changes transformed the Éclat into a car that the press was unanimous in declaring one of the best front-engined Lotuses ever.

The Excel underwent a facelift in 1985, giving rise to the Excel SE and SA models. These gained blisters over the larger 15x7 alloy wheels, and the 2.2-litre Lotus engine was tweaked to give an extra 20bhp, taking the power to a healthy 180bhp, and providing a significant performance boost. The SA version had a new four-speed automatic gearbox supplied by ZF, and helped the car

The rear end of the Excel was neatly laid out and had a big boot spoiler.

Under the bonnet of the Excel sits the 2.2-litre Lotus engine. Fitted with a pair of Dellorto carburettors, the engine produced up to a healthy 180bhp.

cover off the market for luxurious, fast, good handling coupés with a dash of practicality.

The Lotus Excel was arguably the pinnacle of the Lotus design philosophy that had begun with the Elan and Plus 2. Taking the two-door coupé configuration to its logical conclusion, the Excel married the good looks of the Éclat with the reliable components from the Toyota parts bin to produce the ultimate version of the car that had started life as the new Elite. Sporting a Toyota gearbox and all-new rear suspension (with, at long last, disc brakes) the Excel was finally the high quality, reliable, and good looking car Lotus needed.

Lotus Excel SE specification

ENGINE: Lotus 900 series all-alloy, four-cylinder, belt-driven DOHC 16-valve. **Bore and stroke:** 95.28 x 76.2mm; **capacity:** 2174cc; **power:** 180bhp at 6580rpm; **torque:** 165lb/ft at 4800rpm. Twin Dellorto twin-choke carburettors.

The 1991 Excel of Martin Bradbury has a nicely trimmed interior with traditional wood on the dashboard.

Seen at Brands Hatch in 2014, this is an Excel 2.2 from 1988.

GEARBOX: Toyota five-speed manual.
SUSPENSION: Front: Independent by double wishbones, single coil over damper, anti-roll bar; **rear:** Independent, lower wishbone, transverse top link, single coil over damper.
STEERING: Rack and pinion.
BRAKES: Discs all round. **Front:** 10.2in (25.9cm); **rear:** 10.5in (26.67cm). Twin-piston callipers.
WHEELS AND TYRES: Alloy 7Jx15, 195/65VR15.
DIMENSIONS: Length: 173.2in (439.8cm); **width:** 71.5in (181.6cm); **track:** 57.5in (146cm) front and rear; **height:** 47.5in (120.7cm); **wheelbase:** 97.8in (248.3cm).
WEIGHT: 2581lb (1168kg).
PERFORMANCE: Top speed: 131mph (210.8kph); **0-62:** 6.8 seconds.

A lovely 1990 Excel parked up at Brands Hatch in 2014.

A REAL SUPERCAR: THE LOTUS ESPRIT

The Lotus Esprit S1 to S3 (1976 to 1987)

The Lotus Esprit launched the brand into the junior mid-engined supercar league. It was a step up from the Europa, and, with its Giorgetto Giugiaro from ItalDesign wedge-shaped body, it was the epitome of modernism and style when it was introduced in 1976. Its place in history was sealed when a Series 1 debuted in the 1977 James Bond film *The Spy Who Loved Me*, with its transformation into a submarine being one of the more surprising aspects of its film appearance.

The Esprit made a second Bond appearance in the 1981 film *For Your Eyes Only* when an Esprit Turbo in an attractive Bronze shade was Bond's transport in the mountains of Europe. This one had less extravagant modifications – the main one being the fitting of a ski rack on the rear deck.

The Esprit was the replacement for the Europa, and the prototype produced by ItalDesign's Giugiaro was based on a stretched Europa chassis fitted with the then new Lotus 2-litre DOHC, 16-valve, four-cylinder 900 series engine. And therein was the rub – the motoring cognoscenti have always turned up their noses at the Esprit because it only had a four-cylinder engine. So, despite its giant-killing performance, handling and looks being equal if not better than most rivals, cylinder snobbery invests rivals from Ferrari, Maserati and Lamborghini with more kudos.

However exotic its looks, the Esprit was firmly based on Lotus 'best practice' – a glass fibre body sitting on a steel backbone chassis – and featured extensive use of parts from other manufacturers. The independent double wishbone front suspension was derived from the General Motors Opel Asconda parts bin, and the transaxle, which sat behind Lotus' own 2-litre 900 series engine, was a Citroën unit, as seen in the Citroën Maserati.

The spine of the car was the chassis, and this departed from the traditional all folded sheet steel affair by having a tubular rear section. It comprised the standard Lotus design of a central box section backbone with

The first of the Esprits, the retrospectively named S1, came out in 1976 and achieved lasting fame when it appeared in the 1977 James Bond film, The Spy Who Loved Me. Doubling up as a submarine, the Esprit acquitted itself well and gained Lotus the elusive 'Bond' cachet.

The Esprit engine came from Lotus with the 2-litre 900 slant four unit. The Citroën transaxle was the same as that used in the front-engined Citroën Maserati.

a 'T' shaped front end; at the rear there was a tubular space frame forming the engine and transmission cradle. At the front the 'T' was a simple box section extension made from folded sheet steel, which provided a light but stiff structure to carry the front suspension, anti-roll bar and steering rack. The central spine was another box section, to the rear of which was welded the tubular and fabricated steel space frame that carried the engine, transmission and rear suspension. The top end of the rear space frame was formed by a fabricated transverse crossmember that sat behind the engine and above the gearbox, and had a bracket at each end to accept the top of each coil spring and damper unit. The bottom of the space frame had a narrower transverse fabricated crossmember each end, which carried the mounts for the suspension's lower transverse arms. There was a pair of cast aluminium brackets bolted to the engine and transmission unit, which carried the engine mounts and the rear brake callipers.

The front suspension was an independent twin wishbone setup, and used the anti-roll bar as one of the bottom wishbones. The wheel, disc and brake calliper was carried on an upright, and steering was by unassisted rack and pinion. Coil-over shock absorbers provided springing and damping.

The rear suspension followed the layout used in the Europa and the new Elite, with each side served by a long fabricated steel trailing arm connecting the chassis to the bottom of the hub carrier, a transverse arm running from the bottom of the hub carrier to the bottom chassis crossmember, and a combined coil and telescopic damper running from the bottom of the hub carrier to the top chassis crossmember. This meant that the driveshaft was used as the top link of the

The Series 2 Esprit followed the S1 in 1978 and was produced until 1980. This is a 1979 limited edition (number 33 of 100) Commemorative model, in Black and Gold JPS colours to celebrate Lotus winning the 1978 Formula 1 Drivers' and Constructors' Championship.

The Esprit Series 3 arrived in 1981 and was produced through to 1987. This 1983 example was seen at Castle Combe in 2018.

suspension, and so it was of fixed length with Hookes joints at each end to accommodate the suspension movement.

While the system had some advantages, in that it was simple and used the minimum of parts, the use of the driveshafts as the top link could result in the drive interfering with the suspension movement. This was not an issue initially, with the system quite capable of coping with the 160bhp, but would become more critical as power output increased.

At the front the brakes were 9.7in (24.6cm) diameter solid discs with opposed piston callipers. Rear brakes were inboard discs, mounted close to the gearbox. The rear discs were a slightly larger diameter than those at the front, at 10.63in (27cm), due to the need to have enough clearance for the driveshaft flanges rather than for increased performance. GKN 'Wolfrace' five-slot alloy wheels were fitted, with 5½J width and 195/70 VR14 sized tyres on the front, and 7.5J and 205/60 VR14 tyres on the rear.

The engine was the by now familiar 900 series 2-litre DOHC, four-valve unit coded as the type 907. There were a couple of minor modifications made to the Elite unit to adapt it to the mid-engined position of the Esprit. The

The Esprit Turbo burst onto the scene in 1980. This 1982 model is in the metallic bronze used on the second Bond Esprit, which starred in the 1981 film For Your Eyes Only.

The Esprit got a restyle in 1987, with a redesigned bodyshell by Peter Stevens, softening the car's lines and bringing it into the 1990s. This is the 1996 to 1999 four-cylinder GT3 version.

timing marks were moved from the front of the crankshaft to the flywheel, and the water outlet pipe exited sideways rather than straight ahead. The engine was also fitted with new camshafts, which gave a boost to mid-range power and torque. The radiator was sited in a duct in the nose of the car, and coolant ran from the engine to the radiator through pipes placed in the chassis backbone.

The gearbox and final drive was sourced from the Citroën SM, the Maserati-powered coupé, and was a five-speed plus reverse unit. The complete unit was housed in an all alloy casting, with the drive to the wheels taken from the rear of the box. Lotus produced its own unique bellhousing, as using the standard Citroën one with an adapter plate would have added too much length to the engine and transmission unit.

The body followed the practice established with the Elite and Éclat, with a top and bottom half united along a central join, covered with a plastic rubbing strip. While the body structure was designed to use the VARI system to produce the main mouldings, the first Esprits were hand laid-up as production estimates did not expect enough cars would be produced to justify the creation of the VARI system moulds. The VARI system was not used to produce the Esprit body until the Stevens redesign of 1987. The Esprit body had a bulkhead diaphragm placed between the passenger compartment and the engine bay. This bulkhead was built up from three pieces of ⅝ and ¾in thick marine ply with a narrow slot cut in its top to form the rear window, which was bonded in place to provide roll-over protection. The front of the body structure had a glass fibre beam running

The first of the Esprits had razor sharp styling by Giorgetto Giugiaro and was a classic from the word go. This lovely Series 1 was photographed at Goodwood in 2019.

The Series 1 Esprit was Lotus' second mid-engined road car, and was the spiritual successor to the Europa. A focused two-seater sports car, the Esprit would top the Lotus range until 2004 when production eventually ceased.

Back to the spectacular S2 Commemorative Edition Esprit. This shot shows the gold alloy wheels used on the S2.

across it, connecting the scuttle with the A posts. The front bonnet gave access to a luggage space, shared with the spare wheel. The lid was supported on gas struts.

At the back, the rear window lifted up, again supported by gas struts, and gave access to a small (7 cubic feet, 198 litres) luggage compartment at the rear, and the engine oil dipstick. The engine itself was concealed under a secondary lift-out cover. The bumpers front and rear were made from foam-filled polyurethane. The virtually flat bonded-in windscreen was angled at 27.5 degrees, and was swept by a single wiper that utilised a pantograph mechanism to ensure around 85% of the screen was covered. The doors had the side impact protection beams in them, as seen on the Elite, but the Esprit items were made from extruded aluminium, providing a weight saving of around 10lb.

Twin interconnected fuel tanks were positioned low down in front of the rear wheels, with a total capacity of 15 gallons (68 litres). While the cabin ended at the rear edge of the door, a pair of rear windows on the rear panel gave a reasonable three-quarter view through the window slot in the rear bulkhead. The traditional Lotus pop-up headlamps were present at the front of the wedge-shaped nose. Each pop-up pod housed a pair of small round headlamps, one for dip beam, one for main.

While still a strict two-seater, with no room behind the two seats, the Esprit interior was significantly larger than that of the Europa, and, with much longer doors, access to the cabin was much improved. The seats were semi-reclined in style, with built-in headrests, and, while the backrest angle was fixed, they could be moved forwards and backwards, and

With the S2 the Esprit kept most of the striking looks of the S1. This white S2 has the discreet air intakes behind the side window, which helped airflow through the engine bay.

there was a ramp-type adjustment to raise or lower the whole assembly. Up front, the low dash panel sloped upwards towards the windscreen.

The instruments, by Veglia, were presented in a space-age looking binnacle sited on top of the sloping dash panel, with the minor switchgear located in the wings of the binnacle. On the passenger side a lidded glove box sat on the top of the dash. The glove box and the binnacle shared the same fittings, making it easier to configure the car for left- or right-hand drive. The first Esprits were trimmed in a very avant garde green cloth on the doors and seat sides, with chrome trim and red and green tartan inserts for the seat faces.

Just a couple of years after the introduction of the Esprit came the updated Type 79 Series 2, introduced in July 1978. The actual changes were minor. A new, better-integrated front spoiler wrapped around the front of the car under the front bumper, improving the crosswind stability and slightly reducing the Esprit's drag. Behind each rear side window, positioned just ahead of the fuel filler cap, was an air intake that directed air into the engine compartment. In the Series 1 the air was fed into the engine from under the car, and the new vents fed in cleaner, cooler air. The full-size spare wheel of the Series 1 was replaced with a space saver, which gave a bit more luggage space in the front compartment. The rear bumper got bigger light clusters, sourced from the Rover SD1, and the Wolfrace slotted alloy wheels were replaced with Lotus-designed four-spoke items from Speedline. The car also received 'Esprit S2' decals on the rear quarters and the instruments were changed from Veglia to Smiths.

In October 1978, the company announced a limited production run of 100 cars to celebrate Lotus' success in winning the Formula 1 Drivers' and Constructors' championships that year. The cars were in the famous JPS colours, with black paint, gold side

The Series 2 was introduced in 1978 with minor updates and improvements. The striking Black and Gold livery of this JPS. Commemorative Edition S2 is enhanced by the side stripes.

This 1981 S2.2 Esprit was photographed at the NEC Classic Show in 2016. The picture shows how the engine lid hinge was set back into the roofline.

Below: The Esprit Series 3 was launched in 1981, with a galvanised chassis and revised rear suspension from the Turbo. The main external difference from the S2 was the new wraparound bumpers, with 'LOTUS' embossed into the rear bumper.

stripes and wheels, and with 'World Champion' incorporated in the side stripe.

The Type 79 Series 2.2 Esprit was introduced in April 1980, and was fitted with the new Type 912 engine, with its larger 2174cc capacity. At the same time the car got a galvanised chassis for better corrosion resistance, and, of course, 'Series 2.2' badges.

Lotus took the lessons learned and the styling revisions made to the Turbo Esprit and applied them to the normally aspirated model, creating the Type 85 Series 3 Esprit in 1981.

Pictured on the historic Brooklands banking in January 2018, this view of a 1983 Esprit S3 shows the new front bumper and spoiler as well as the 'esprit 3' badging on the bonnet.

The major change was the adoption of the Turbo's galvanised chassis, which meant the car adopted the Turbo style rear suspension, with its short top links and driveshafts that were now not used as parts of the suspension. As the driveshafts were now independent of the suspension, they had to be splined (plunger linked) to allow for changes in length when the suspension moved.

The black front spoiler sills and valance of the Series 2.2 were now body colour, and the rear bumper had 'LOTUS' moulded into it between the rear light units, leaving following drivers in no doubt as to what had just overtaken them.

The Series 3 Esprit was long-lived, being made from 1981 through to 1987.

Lotus Esprit S1 specification

ENGINE: Lotus 911 all alloy four-cylinder, belt driven DOHC, 16-valve. **Bore and stroke:** 95.28 x 69.24; **capacity:** 1973cc; **power:** 156bhp at 6580rpm; **torque:** 140lb/ft at 4800rpm. Twin Weber twin-choke carburettors.
GEARBOX: Citroën five-speed transaxle.
SUSPENSION: Front: Independent by double wishbones, single coil-over damper. Anti-roll bar. **Rear:** Independent, driveshaft top link, trailing arm bottom link and transverse link. Coil-over dampers.
STEERING: Rack and pinion.
BRAKES: Discs all round. **Front:** 9.7in (24.6cm); **rear:** 10.63in (26.9cm). Twin-piston callipers.
WHEELS AND TYRES: Wheels: 6Jx14 front; 7Jx14 rear. **Tyres:** 1195/70 HR 14 front, 205/70 HR 14 rear.
DIMENSIONS: Length: 165in (419.1cm); **width:** 73.3in (186.2cm); **track:** 59.5in (151.1cm) front and rear; **height:** 43in (109.2cm); **wheelbase:** 96in (243.8cm).
WEIGHT: 2015lb (914kg).
PERFORMANCE: Top speed: 138mph (201kph); **0-60:** 6.8 seconds.

The Lotus Type 82 Esprit Turbo (1980 to 1987)

While the Lotus Esprit had great looks, a mid-mounted engine and good performance from the naturally aspirated Lotus 907 series engine, it was not quite enough to be top of the junior supercar pile. The best way of getting more useable power from an engine in the 1980s was by turbocharging, and the Esprit was the perfect candidate. With its already good handling, light weight and relatively roomy engine bay the car was crying out for more performance, and the Esprit Turbo provided it. The original 1973cc 907 series fitted to the Esprit was redesigned and became the 910 unit, with a capacity increase to 2174cc, a dry sump oil system and a Garrett AiResearch turbocharger. This was fitted behind the cylinder block and above the gearbox bellhousing, and boosted power output to 210bhp at 6250rpm. The

The Esprit Turbo was released in 1980. A limited edition was produced in the colours of Essex Petroleum, Lotus' racing sponsor. The distinctive blue with red and grey stripes made the Essex Esprit a distinctive and attractive car with supercar performance.

The Esprit Turbo gained some aerodynamic tweaks, including deeper sill covers with NACA-style ducts at the rear of the sill to increase airflow into the engine bay. The new wheels were 15in diameter three-piece alloy Compomotives.

From the front the most distinctive feature of the new Turbo Esprit was the new design for the nose badge.

extra power meant a larger diameter clutch was needed.

The front suspension gained bigger front discs (sourced from the top-of-the-range Opel Asconda) and the rear suspension reworked, with the addition of short top links from the hub to the chassis. This meant the driveshafts no longer formed the top link of the suspension, and were fitted with sliding splines to take up the changes in length as the suspension moved. The rear cradle was modified to fit in the new dry sump engine and to fit brackets to take the new top links for the revised rear suspension. The front 'box' onto which the suspension mounted was also stiffened, and the whole chassis was now galvanised to give excellent corrosion resistance. The changes to the chassis were claimed to increased the torsional stiffness by 50%.

The new Type 82 Esprit Turbo was announced in February 1980 at a lavish party at London's Royal Albert Hall, hosted by Lotus' then Formula One Sponsor, Essex Petroleum. At the launch of the new car a limited edition version, the Essex Commemorative Edition, was also launched. This limited edition version of the car was in blue with the 'Essex' logo printed on red and silver side stripes. Despite

The 15in Compomotive wheels fill the wheelarches of this 1982 model. The 'turbo esprit' graphics leave no doubt as to the nature of the car.

The nose graphics let people know in no uncertain terms that this is a Turbo Esprit. With its deep front spoiler and wrap around front bumper the Esprit is every inch a supercar.

the February launch customer cars only started to be delivered in August.

The new car had some subtle restyling when compared with the then current normally aspirated Series 2.2 Esprit. The body received a new louvred panel over the engine cover, and the front spoiler was stretched so it sat all the way across the front of the car and splayed out along the edge to the front wheelarch, under a new wraparound front bumper. The splayed-out lines of the front spoiler continued on in the sill extensions that ran between the front and rear wheels, below the door. A NACA-style duct on the rear of each sill directed air into the engine bay.

The air ducts first seen on the S2, behind the side windows, were extended upwards to integrate with a subtle little spoiler across the roof, just ahead of the hinge line of the rear panel. An additional, large spoiler was added to the tail of the car. This did no favours for the drag, supposedly added some downforce to the tail, and made it obvious that the car was a sporting number!

In 1983 the dry sump lubrication system was replaced with a conventional wet sump. Then, in 1986, the Turbo Esprit HC and HCPI was introduced. The HCPI was US market specific, and the HC was for the 'rest of the world' markets.

The HC gave the Esprit a power boost, with a higher compression ratio of 8:1 and increased boost – up from 8psi to 9.5psi. Along with a change to a pair of Dellorto DHLA 45mm carburettors, this meant the engine had a 20% uplift in power to 215bhp at 6250rpm, and a 10% uplift in torque to 220lb/ft at 4250rpm. Upgraded exhaust manifolds, a new casting for the turbocharger, and increased cooling capacity finished off the improvements.

Developments of the US market HPCI cars led to the introduction of Bosch K-Jetronic fuel injection systems, along with a closed loop catalyst to meet ever more stringent emissions legislation.

White was always a popular choice of colour for the Esprit thanks to the car's appearance in the Bond film The Spy Who Loved Me. This lovely 1986 example was pictured at Brands Hatch in 2014.

This 1983 example was photographed in 2016 at the Club Lotus track day at Castle Combe circuit. The front three-quarter view shows the NACA ducts on the sills and the Compomotive split rim alloy wheels. The rear three-quarter view shows the rear bumper and the Rover SD1 rear lights.

A unique feature of the Turbo Esprit was the four-slat panel that sat above the engine bay lid.

From the front the main way to distinguish a Turbo Esprit from the normally aspirated model are the nose graphics.

Lotus Esprit Turbo specification

ENGINE: Lotus 910 all alloy four-cylinder, belt-driven DOHC, 16-valve. **Bore and stroke:** 95.28 x 76.2; **capacity:** 2174cc; **power:** 210bhp at 6000rpm; **torque:** 200lb/ft at 4000rpm. Twin Weber twin-choke carburettors.
GEARBOX: Citroën five-speed transaxle.
SUSPENSION: Front: Independent by double wishbones, single coil over damper, anti-roll bar; **rear:** Independent, driveshaft top link, trailing arm bottom link and transverse link. Coil over dampers.
STEERING: Rack and pinion.
BRAKES: Discs all round. 10.5in (26.67cm) diameter, twin-piston callipers.
WHEELS AND TYRES: Wheels: Alloys, front 7J, rear 8J. **Tyres:** 195/60VR15 front, 235/60 VR15 rear.
DIMENSIONS: Length: 165in (419.1cm); **width:** 73.3in (186.2cm); **track:** 60.5in (153.67cm) front, 61.2in (155.5cm) rear; **height:** 44in (111.76cm); **wheelbase:** 96in (243.8cm).
WEIGHT: 2015lb (914kg).
PERFORMANCE: Top speed; 138mph (201kph); **0-60:** 6.8 seconds.

The 1987 restyle of the Esprit by Peter Stevens resulted in a much softer design. Pictured at Brands Hatch in 2014 this 1996 V8-powered example shows its five-spoke alloy wheels and the large rear spoiler.

The Stevens Esprit, Esprit Turbo and Esprit V8 (1987 to 1993)

The Esprit received a styling update in 1987, softening its sharp, 1970s Giugiaro lines, and bringing the car's looks completely up to date. The new look was penned by designer Peter Stevens, and the car was labelled the X180. By keeping the Esprit's underpinnings the same, the company was able to design and develop the 'new' car in only 15 months, with deliveries to customers beginning as soon as the car was announced in October 1987. The bodyshell had Kevlar reinforcement in the roof and sides to provide enhanced roll-over protection and was manufactured using the VARI process. One feature the new car gained was a roof panel that could be opened slightly to improve ventilation, or removed completely and stored in the rear boot.

Other changes across the range was the inclusion of a new Renault sourced transaxle (also used in the Alpine GTA), which also meant the original inboard rear discs were moved outboard. The restyled car was available in both normally aspirated and turbocharged guise. In normally aspirated form the cars had the 172bhp version of the 2.2-litre engine, and the side sills and front spoiler were body coloured.

This selection of Stevens Esprits shows the softer lines that gave the car a modern look.

The normally aspirated car would be dropped from the range in 1992, after which all the four-cylinder Esprit variants were turbocharged. The turbo versions of the new Stevens cars now had electronic fuel injection, and had dark metallic silver grey finish on the side sills, front spoiler and rear valance, plus different alloy wheels.

In 1989 the Esprit Turbo SE was launched, with a new Delco engine management system, twin-coil distributor-less ignition system, and a new super efficient inter cooling system dubbed 'Chargecooling'. These changes boosted power to 264bhp and 261lb/ft, and the car was produced up to 1993.

In 1992 Lotus introduced the Esprit Sport 300, which was the final iteration of the four-cylinder Esprit Turbo family. The engine was ported, had larger intake and exhaust valves, a new turbocharger, and a recalibrated ECU, all of which gave 302bhp at 6400rpm. The aim was to produce a track-focused car with a top speed of 162mph and a 0-60 time of just 4.5 seconds. To save weight the car had a modified version of the old S3 Esprit body, which had wheelarch extensions to cover the wider wheels.

In January 1993 Lotus introduced the Esprit S4. It used the new-style Stevens bodyshell and had power assisted steering for the first time on the Esprit.

1994 saw the introduction of the S4S, followed in 1996 by the GT3, a budget 2-litre turbo car producing 240bhp. Then, in 1996, came the ultimate version of the Esprit: the Esprit V8. Lotus' new V8 was not a development of the old 900 series engine, it was a completely new design despite its '918' design designation, and was a 3506cc 90-degree V8 with four belt-driven overhead camshafts, four valves per cylinder, and twin Garrett turbochargers. The V8GT arrived in December 1997, and the V8SE came in 1998.

The rarest of the Esprit V8s was the lightweight Esprit Sport 350 of 1998-2001; followed in 1998 by the Esprit Sport 350, another twin-turbo V8 producing a claimed 350bhp. It was fitted with a different ECU to alter the engine's power delivery, as well as having chassis, body and brake upgrades. The last of the Esprit line was aptly called the Esprit 'Final Edition', and just 82 such cars were built between 2002 and 2004.

This Stevens Esprit Sport 350 is powered by the Lotus V8 engine. Only 54 Sport 350s were produced, between 1998 and 2001.

The Stevens Esprit S4 was produced between 1993 and 1995. Powered by a turbocharged four-cylinder engine, the car had some 264bhp.

This Esprit S4 was pictured at Brands Hatch in 2014. The size of the rear hatch is apparent.

Lotus Esprit V8 specification

ENGINE: Lotus 918 all alloy V8, belt-driven four overhead camshafts, 32 valves. **Bore and stroke:** 83mm x 81mm; **capacity:** 3506cc; **power:** 350bhp at 6500rpm; **torque:** 295lb/ft at 4250rpm. Twin turbochargers.
GEARBOX: Renault five-speed transaxle.
SUSPENSION: Front: Independent by double wishbones, single coil-over damper, anti-roll bar; **rear:** Independent, driveshaft top link, trailing arm bottom link and transverse link. Coil-over dampers.
STEERING: Rack and pinion.
BRAKES: Ventilated discs all round. **Front:** 11.6in (29.5cm); **rear:** 11.8in (30.0cm). Opposed piston callipers.
WHEELS AND TYRES: Wheels: Alloys, 7J front, 8J rear. **Tyres:** 235/40ZR17 front, 285/35ZR18 rear.
DIMENSIONS: Length: 172in (436.9cm); **width:** 73.3in (186.2cm); **track:** 60.2in (152.9cm) front, 60.8in (154.4cm) rear; **height:** 45.3in (115.1cm); **wheelbase:** 96in (243.8cm).
WEIGHT: 3045lb (1381kg).
PERFORMANCE: Top speed: 175mph (201kph); **0-60:** 4.1 seconds.

The 1996 to 1999 GT3 Esprit was powered by a 2-litre version of the Lotus four-cylinder engine, producing 240bhp. It was cheaper to buy than the upcoming V8, but still delivered good performance.

THE NEW LOTUS ELAN

The Lotus type 100 Elan (also known as the 'M100 Elan') of 1989 resurrected the name of arguably Lotus' finest road car. The M100 followed Lotus practice of using a glass reinforced plastic body and backbone chassis, but broke tradition by using a proprietary engine and gearbox and having front-wheel drive. If this was not enough, the cars that Peter Stevens penned were also controversial, with a 'cab forward' appearance. This made the car look shorter and wider than it actually was, and not at all the sleek and sporty look that fans felt a Lotus should have.

Despite this negativity the car was actually very good; it was praised by the press and road testers of the time, and won an award from the UK Design Council. However, sales were relatively poor and the car did not survive for long. Production ceased in 1992, but, when Bugatti took over production was restarted for a second batch of some 800 cars badged 'S2', for Series 2, and production finally ceased in September 1995. There was a surprise ending to the M100 saga: after the final S2 cars were produced, Lotus sold the design to Kia, which introduced its re-engined version in 1996 for the Korean market. Production of the Kia M100 ended in 2000.

Lotus Elan M100 (1989 to 1995)

A small two-seat sports car with a soft top and reasonable sized boot, the M100 dipped deep into GM's parts bin.

Despite Lotus' fruitful and mutually beneficial relationship with Toyota, forged in the early 1980s, GM had bought a majority share in Lotus in 1985, and instigated a major investment programme for the company. Part of this programme granted access to the company's global resources; a major plus point of the relationship. In the late 1980s, the Lotus range was ageing, comprising just the Excel and Esprit, and a new model was needed to rejuvenate the range and the company. So the engineers at Lotus looked back to their former glory and decided to reprieve the Elan, but in a format appropriate to the modern times.

Mike Kimberley was quoted in an article in *Car and Driver* magazine as saying that the company opted for a front-wheel drive as the best choice for a sports car of this size and power, and added that it didn't want to be seen to be making just another Toyota MR2, which rather ruled out a mid-engined design. In addition, the company didn't want its new product to have a backwards looking design, so this precluded the front engine, rear-wheel drive format seen on the Elan and the Mazda

The M100 was a replacement for the much loved Elan – a small agile two-seat sports car. Here a small group enjoys the sunshine at Castle Combe circuit in 2012.

The M100 was a small two-seater – this profile view shows its stubby lines, which were quite unlike any former Lotus model.

MX5. The end result was that the car would be front-wheel drive, and, from the GM parts bin, the best choice of engine and transmission was found in the Isuzu Gemini. This engine and gearbox, which in the Lotus application was coded 4XE1, was a front-wheel drive application, but could have lent itself to a mid-engined layout except that had already been ruled out. As the car had to be front-wheel drive, Lotus' own suspension engineers – pre-eminent in their field – had to devise a way of making the new car drive as well as a rear-wheel drive car.

The fundamental issue was that front-wheel drive could corrupt the steering feel – in a rear-wheel drive car the front wheels move with the suspension and steering inputs, while the rear wheels transmit the power to the road. In a front-wheel drive car the front end has to handle the suspension and steering inputs, feed in the power, and cope with the majority of the weight of the drivetrain sitting on the front wheels. This usually leads to effects such as torque steer, heavy steering and resistance to steering inputs, all of which conspire to corrupt the steering feel, while the rear end simply follows along behind. Lotus wanted to divorce the effects of putting the power through the front wheels from the steering and achieved this by mounting the front suspension on an isolating 'raft'.

While Lotus used the standard Isuzu engine and gearbox mounts, it added an extra engine mount at the rear of the engine to help to prevent it rocking, which also helped to eliminate unwanted input to the steering and suspension. By all accounts the M100's steering function was not influenced by the power input at all, and made the M100 probably the best feeling front-wheel drive car ever.

To sum up, the M100 Elan was a two-seat, soft top, front-wheel drive sports car, with a steel chassis and glass fibre bodywork, and was offered to the market in two versions: the normally aspirated Elan and the turbocharged Elan SE.

While the M100 chassis adopted the standard Lotus backbone approach, the mounting of the engine and gearbox with its associated drive components meant that the complete package was rather more complex.

The main chassis was fabricated from sheet steel, with a box section central part that extended up to the front axle line. There were steel reinforcement panels added to the main chassis to form the sills, front scuttle and windscreen hoop, the A and B posts, and the rear scuttle, along with reinforcing beams in the doors, all of which combined to form a rigid safety cell around the passengers. At the front of the main chassis there was a substantial crossmember, and to this was bolted a front frame.

The first generation of the M100, retrospectively known as a Series 1 car, was produced between 1989 and 1992. This is Martin Houston's 1990 example.

The front frame comprised a pair of longitudinal arms, a front crossmember and a central structure, which sat under and behind the engine unit and was mounted on the main chassis crossmember, nicknamed the 'prongeron'. The front frame carried the complete engine/gearbox/final drive unit, as well as the tops of the front strut towers, and also formed the main crash energy absorbing structure.

To help isolate the chassis from suspension input, the front suspension mounts, apart from the tops of the struts, were carried on a pair of separate cast alloy rafts. The rear of each raft was rubber-mounted to the main chassis crossmember, the front rubber-mounted on the 'prongeron', and the top rubber-mounted on the strut tower. The front suspension was by twin unequal length wishbones with the bottom of the suspension strut bolted to the lower wishbone using a 'U' shaped yoke to equalise loads on the wishbone and give clearance for the driveshaft. The upper and lower wishbones were bolted directly onto the raft using stiff bushes, and the anti-roll bar was mounted on the front lower wishbone at the strut yoke. The front hub was a light alloy unit, bolted to the top and bottom wishbones using swivel joints.

At the rear the suspension was similar to

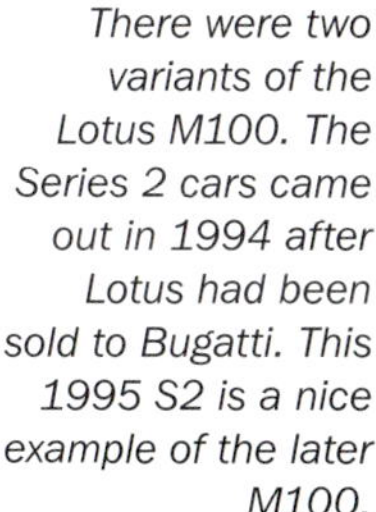

There were two variants of the Lotus M100. The Series 2 cars came out in 1994 after Lotus had been sold to Bugatti. This 1995 S2 is a nice example of the later M100.

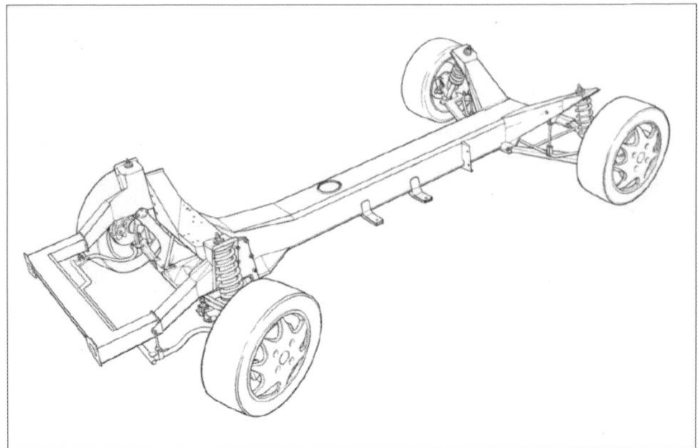

The basic M100 chassis was made of steel and was a backbone design, similar to that used in the Elan and the Elite families of cars.

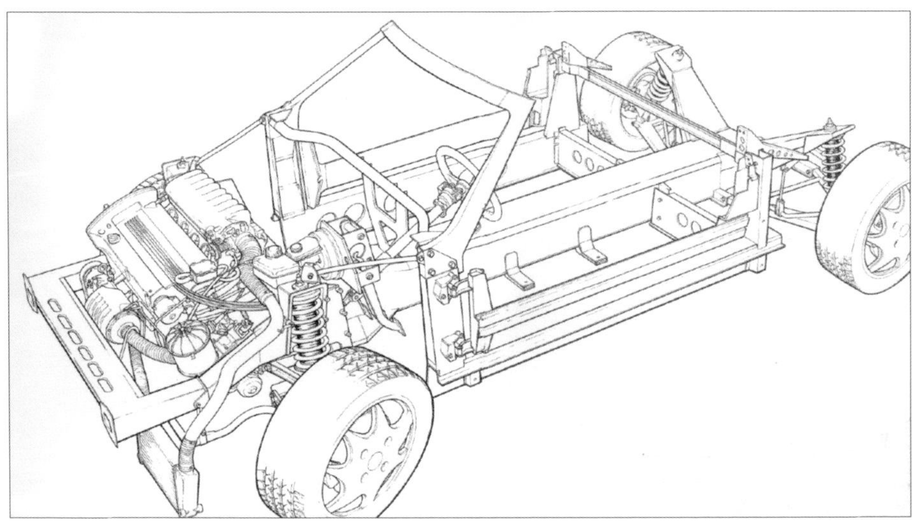

The M100 chassis had a substantial steel superstructure added to enhance passenger protection and add stiffness to the basic backbone. This included the windscreen surround and A and B posts. Note also the door reinforcing beam.

the original Elan's layout, with a singe lower wide-based wishbone and a strut to carry the hub, but also had a top link to control wheel camber, plus an anti-roll bar.

Brakes were discs all round, with the 10in (25.4cm) diameter ventilated front rotors mounted on the hub carrier, and the solid 9.3in (23.6cm) diameter rear rotors mounted outboard on the hub. The wheels were 6.5x15 alloys, shod with 205/50 profile tyres.

In the Lotus application the Isuzu unit was bored out from its original 1500cc to have almost square bore and stroke of 80mm x 79mm and a capacity of 1588cc. The unit gained a strengthened (cast iron) cylinder block, lightened connecting rods, new camshafts, and the 16-valve head was modified to have pent roof combustion chambers.

In normally aspirated form the compression ratio was 9.8.1, and produced a healthy 135bhp at 7200rpm and 103lb/ft of torque at 5600rpm. The turbocharged version had a CR of 8.5:1, and produced 165bhp at 6600rpm and peak torque of 148lb/ft at 4200rpm. The cam covers carried joint

Under the M100's bonnet sits a transversely mounted Isuzu 1600 engine and gearbox.

Isuzu-Lotus branding with the writing in the respective company fonts.

The M100 Elan's bodyshell was made from glass reinforced plastic, and was produced using a variant of the VARI process. However the process differed from that of the Elite/Éclat/Excel/Esprit by being made up of 63 different panels. These panels were then combined together in a jig on the production line. The process also allowed for the use of different panel designs for specific markets. The M100's body was largely unstressed so the panels were usually only around 2mm thick, although there were some with local strengthening up to 4mm thick.

Designed by Simon Cox, the M100's interior, unsurprisingly, also relied on the GM parts bin, including the instrument cluster, minor instruments, as well as the switch gear and stalks. However, the whole interior was

The M100 has the classic pop-up headlights, rarely seen open except in the dark!

The front end of Martin Houston's M100 shows the classic Lotus styling feature of pop-up headlamps, making for a very smooth nose.

The M100 interior was very nicely integrated and looked great. Despite using mainly GM switches and instruments Lotus made the design its own.

particularly well integrated, and, with new leather-covered seats, door cards and centre console, the result was a modern and really rather pleasant driving environment.

The M100's fabric hood was designed by Tickford, and was manually operated, folding down into a compartment ahead of the boot, and covered by a rigid, flush-fitting panel when down.

At the front the pop-up headlamps underwent a rapid redesign when the first iteration presented some issues in service. The complex design had the lights facing upwards under their covers when at rest, then they would fold forwards when they came up. The system was found to be noisy in operation, complex to make and maintain, and dazzled oncoming drivers as the lights pivoted into

From this angle, Martin's M100 Elan shows the 'cab forward' look, a defining feature of the M100. The car did not gain the sales Lotus hoped for, but not due to any dynamic shortfalls.

The rear view shows the M100's main styling issue – the car was surprisingly wide, which contributed to its excellent handling and roadholding but did make it look a bit squat.

The S2 cars had 16in diameter wheels and the range was given two new colours. This example is finished in Medina, a metallic sea green.

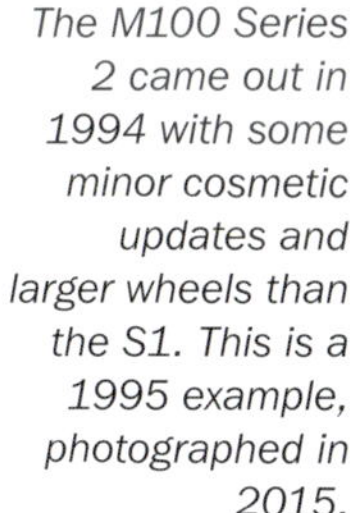

The M100 Series 2 came out in 1994 with some minor cosmetic updates and larger wheels than the S1. This is a 1995 example, photographed in 2015.

This S2 shows the second new colour introduced for the S2, a deep metallic purple named Palacio. In this car's case it is set off nicely by a white interior.

Kia bought the rights to the design of the M100 and produced the car between 1997 and 1990 for the Korean market with the name Vigato. This is a brochure shot of the Kia.

position. They were replaced with a simpler design based on the single-pivot pods found on the Excel and Esprit.

A decent-sized boot finished off what was really a very accomplished package. However, despite the rave reviews, the undoubted dynamic effectiveness, and reasonable price the new Elan struggled to gain sales against the opposition – the main one being the cheaper, more conventional, and good-looking Mazda MX5.

The first iteration of the M100 sold 3855 cars before GM pulled the plug on production in 1992. Of these cars only 129 were the normally aspirated models, and 559 units were sold in the USA.

As mentioned above, production restarted under Bugatti's ownership with 800 Series 2 cars produced between 1994 and 1995, which were broadly similar to the original cars but had larger 16in wheels and a catalytic converter. Finally, there were 729 Kia models produced for the Korean home market between 1996 and 2000. Named the Vigato, the car was powered by Kia's own 1793cc normally aspirated DOHC four-cylinder engine that produced 135bhp at 6250rpm.

Lotus Type 100 Elan specification

ENGINE: GM/Isuzu straight-four, DOHC 16-valve. **Normally aspirated:** Compression ratio of 9.8:1 giving 130bhp at 5200rpm and 105lb/ft of torque at 4200rpm; **Turbocharged:** compression ratio of 8.5:1 giving 165bhp at 6600rpm and 148lb/ft of torque at 4200rpm.
GEARBOX: Front-wheel drive, five-speed Isuzu manual.
SUSPENSION: Front: Independent by double unequal length wishbones, anti-roll bar; **rear:** Independent, broad-based bottom wishbone, top links, anti-roll bar.
STEERING: Rack and pinion.
BRAKES: Discs all round. **Front:** 10in (24.5cm); **rear:** 9.3in (23.6cm).
WHEELS AND TYRES: Wheels: Five-spoke 6.5x15in; **tyres:** 205/50 ZR 15.
DIMENSIONS: Length: 149.75in (380cm); **width:** 74.3in (188.6cm); **height:** 48.4in (122.8cm); **wheelbase:** 88.6in (224.9cm).
WEIGHT: 2276lb (1032kg).
PERFORMANCE: Normally aspirated top speed: 122mph (196kph); **0-60:** 7.6 seconds; **Turbo top speed:** 137mph (220kph); **0-60:** 6.7 seconds.

NEW AGE, NEW TECH, NEW RANGE

With the announcement of the Elise in 1995 Lotus entered a completely new era. The Elise was as ground-breaking as the Elan had been in 1963, and, just like the Elan with its folded steel backbone chassis and glass fibre body, marked the introduction of a completely new architecture that would underpin all the company's designs for the next three decades. The Elise was based on an aluminium platform chassis made by glueing and riveting aluminium extrusions and sheet together to form a rigid but lightweight structure. The new chassis architecture could be easily changed to make longer or wider structures, and, in fact, Lotus licensed the technology to Aston Martin, resulting in the 'VH' range of cars, starting with the DB9 of 2004.

The Lotus Type 111 Elise (1996 to 2021)

The Lotus Elise was the car that gave Lotus back its mojo. Launched at the Frankfurt Motor Show in September 1995 and going on sale in 1996, the Elise was a small, lightweight, mid-engined, two-seat sports car with no frills but a bucketful of innovative features. The car had great performance and exemplary handing and roadholding, and was every inch a Lotus.

After relying on the formula of a steel backbone and glass fibre bodyshell for many years, with the Elise Lotus branched off in a completely new and innovative direction. The basis of the Elise was an all aluminium platform chassis, built up from extruded aluminium forms and sheet aluminium fixed together using glue (and some rivets) to form a rigid, lightweight structure. This was known

The Elise was the car that regained Lotus' reputation for producing lightweight, agile great performing cars. The backbone of the Elise was its new platform chassis made from lightweight aluminium extrusions.

The first Elise was an attractive little sports car. A strict two-seater, this is Andrew Wooley's Series 1.

With glass fibre bodywork shrouding the platform chassis, the Elise is small and delicate. The open cabin gives 'wind in the hair' motoring.

The Elise cabin is stark and functional but still attractive in a minimalist sense. The wide sills and neat instrument binnacle are evident.

as Lotus' 'Small Platform' chassis, and would form the basis of a range of cars, the first of which was the Elise.

The Elise's bodywork was minimal, with glass fibre clamshells front and rear and minimal paneling for the two-seat cabin. The doors were small and light, windows were wound up and down by hand, and the roof was a detachable panel sitting between the top of the windscreen frame and the built-in rollover hoop that also provided the frame for the rear screen.

The interior was stark, with no carpets, just bare aluminium highlighting the fundamental structure of the car, and had minimal creature comforts. Information was fed to the driver by a small instrument binnacle, appropriately designed by the stylish but minimalist Philippe Starck, perched on the top of the driver's side dash. The instruments provided the basic information the driver needed simply and clearly, with an analogue speedometer and rev counter backed up with LCD displays for other functions.

Following the example set with the M100 Elan, the Elise used a proprietary engine and transmission unit, and the Elise was initially powered by a Rover K series unit and had a five-speed manual gearbox also from the Rover parts bin – a package similar to that seen in the mid-engined MG TF of 1995. The K series

The rear of the Elise shows off its pert lines. A simple pair of round rear lights echoes the Series 1 Elan.

Under the engine cover sits a 1.8-litre Rover 'K' Series engine and transmission. This peppy little DOHC unit fits perfectly with the Elise's ethos of a fast light and agile sports car.

From any angle the Elise is a pretty sports car, and the looks are unique to Lotus. Note the open roof and built-in roll-over hoop.

engine was actually a little jewel of an engine, a state of the art, well-proven lightweight, all alloy, straight four, DOHC 16-valve unit which, even in normally aspirated form, could pump out close to 100bhp per litre.

Early iterations of the unit used in the Rover Metro and MG F/MG TF had problems with head gasket failure caused by poorly located head gaskets causing coolant loss and subsequent head warping when the engine overheated. However the Elise version did not seem to suffer from this malaise and when properly maintained the unit gives good reliable service. In the Elise the unit displaced 1796cc and produced 118bhp and 120lb/ft of torque.

Suspension-wise, the Elise was more conventional than its chassis, with double wishbones and rack and pinion steering up front, and a fully independent double wishbone setup at the rear. There were disc brakes all round which were made from lightweight metal matrix material, and the car had minimal overhangs giving it a 'wheel at each corner' look that emphasised the car's impeccable handing and roadholding.

The Elise re-established Lotus at the top of the sports car manufacturers' tree. It was an uncompromising car, aimed at transporting two people quickly and efficiently from a to b as fast and as safely as possible. It achieved this aim by being lightweight, having superlative handling and grip, and enabling a skilled driver to extract maximum satisfaction by exploiting the beautifully balanced combination of power and handing.

The Elise range is comprised of a wide range of models, which can lead to confusion and a lack of clarity as to which model came out when. There isn't enough room in the book to give a detailed description of all of the changes, model-by-model, so this is an overview of the models and their main characteristics.

The Lotus Elise was introduced at the 1995 Frankfurt Motor Show, the standard Elise went on sale in the UK in 1996 and was in production until 2000. The Sport Elise Sprint 190 was introduced in March 1997, and the Sport 135 was introduced in 1998. Then in 1999 the 143bhp Elise 111S was introduced, with the final Series 1 models, the

From the front the Elise's pair of round indicators recall the Lotus Europa. Here the fabric hood is in place to provide a modicum of weather protection.

Three generations of Elise in one shot: the Series 1 is in the centre, with the Series 2 to the right and the Series 3 on the left.

Sport 160 and Sport 190 variants added in 2000.

The Elise S2 was launched in October 2000 at the Birmingham Motor Show. With a redesigned soft top and slightly larger luggage capacity, plus lowered chassis side rails and better side windows, the restyled Elise was easier to live with than the original. The car still relied on the excellent 1796cc Rover K series engine, was slightly longer and wider than the original, and, with various aerodynamic improvements, the Elise S2 gave slightly better performance while still retaining the outstanding roadholding and handling of the original. The first variant of the Series 2 was the 135R introduced in 2001, and this was followed in 2002 by the 111S with Rover K Series VVC engine.

Jennie Lawrence's 2019 Series 3 Elise. Slightly larger than the original, the car still retains all the Elise's benefits.

The sport Elise 135R was introduced in 2003, and 2004 saw the Federal Elise going on sale in the USA, and the 111R with 189bhp made available in the UK and Europe. In 2004 the venerable Rover K series engine was replaced with the 1.8-litre Toyota ZZ four-cylinder DOHC unit and its six-speed gearbox. The Elise 111R was introduced in 2005, and then in 2007 the Elise S was released, and the Elise 111R was renamed the Elise R. For 2008 the range comprised the Elise S (134bhp), the Elise R (189bhp) and the supercharged Elise SC (218bhp). In 2011 there was a facelift, with the cars sometimes being referred to as the Series 3, with a new front clamshell with new headlights and air intakes.

The next changes came in 2013 with the introduction of the Elise S Club Racer and Elise Cup R track cars, and the following year

With its fabric roof in place, Jennie Lawrence's Elise Series 3 basks in the summer sun.

First up in a row of modern Lotus models, the Series 3 Elise is a simply lovely sports car.

saw the Elise S Cup. In 2016 the Elise 250 Special Edition and Elise Race 250 models were introduced, and in 2020 the final Elise variants, the Classic Heritage Editions, were introduced. These final limited edition Elises had colour schemes based on the Lotus Formula 1 team colours, including the classic British Racing Green and yellow, the Gold Leaf Team Lotus red over white, and the black and gold John Player Special. In 2017 Lotus announced the Elise Sprint, lightweight versions of the standard car. Production of the Elise ended in the early 2020s, with the 2021 announcement of the run out Elise Sport 240 and the Cup 250 Final Edition.

Lotus Type 111 Elise specification

ENGINE: Rover K Series all aluminium straight-four, DOHC, 16-valve. **Bore and stroke:** 80mm x 89.3mm; **capacity:** 1796cc; 118bhp at 5500rpm; **torque:** 122lb/ft at 4800.

GEARBOX: Rover five-speed.

SUSPENSION: Front: Independent by double wishbones, single coil-over damper, anti-roll bar; **rear:** Independent, by double wishbones, single coil-over damper.

STEERING: Rack and pinion.

BRAKES: Aluminium matrix ventilated discs all round. 11.1in (28.2cm) diameter, AP twin-piston callipers.

DIMENSIONS: Length: 146.7in (372.6cm); **width:** 67in (170.2cm); **track:** 56.7in (144cm) front, 57.2 (145.3cm) rear; **height:** 47.3in (120.1cm); **wheelbase:** 90.6in (230.1cm).

WEIGHT: 1488lb (675kg).

PERFORMANCE: Top speed: 124mph (201kph); **0-62:** 5.9 seconds.

Lotus Type 111 Exige (2000 to 2021)

Sticking with an existing Type number, a major version of the Type 111 was the Exige. Introduced in 2000, the Exige was a closed coupé version of the Elise and the new car combined many parts from the Elise family to produce a hardcore sporting coupé with excellent performance, handling and roadholding. The original Exige was aimed at a much more sporting clientele then the Elise, and came with a fixed roof, and a body style derived from the Series 1 Elise. The most noticeable difference from the Elise was the roof-mounted engine air intake, a pylon mounted rear wing, and the widened bodywork to accommodate the increase in track. Like the Elise there were many Exige models, usually made in limited numbers and over relatively short time periods. The following is a brief overview of the model's lifespan.

The Exige S1 was introduced in 2000, and was still powered by the 1.8-litre DOHC Rover K series engine, but in Very High Performance Derivative (VHPD) form, giving a healthy 177bhp and mated with a five-speed gearbox. This was followed in 2004 by the Exige Series 2, which was now powered by the 189bhp Toyota 2ZZ-GE motor, fitted with a six-speed gearbox and styled like the Series 2 Elise. In 2005 a supercharged limited edition of 50 Sport Exige R was introduced, and in 2006 the Exige S was launched. The Exige S had its Toyota four-cylinder engine supercharged to deliver 220bhp, and the Exige went on sale in the US. The 240bhp Exige S 240 went on sale in 2008, along with the track day/competition Exige GT3, and in 2012 the Exige S Roadster was introduced.

The Toyota V6-powered Series 3 Exige was introduced in 2012 at the Frankfurt motor show in the shape of the Exige S V6 with supercharged Toyota V6 engine giving 345bhp. This was followed in 2013 by the roadster version, which had a detachable top. From 2013 the track-oriented Exige V6 Cup and track-only V6 Cup R were produced. Lotus celebrated its F1 success with a limited edition of 81 Exige LF1s, finished in JPS black and gold. Then in 2016 came the Exige 350 Special edition of 50 cars. More Cup editions arrived in 2017, with the Exige Race 380, Cup 380 and Cup 430, followed in 2018 by the Cup 430 Type 25, the Sport 410, and Exige Type 49 and Type 79. The final year of Exige production was 2021, with the Exige Sport 410 Twentieth Anniversary model.

The Exige was a more track focused version of the Elise. With its closed cabin and air intake on the roof it has a distinctive look that separates it from the Elise.

The Exige's air scoop and the different front bodywork mark the car out as a more raw alternative to the Elise.

The Exige's back end sports a large spoiler on stilts. Otherwise the back end is very similar to the Elise.

Lotus Exige S2 specification

ENGINE: Toyota 2ZZ-GE, four-cylinder DOHC 16-valve VVTL (Variable Valve Timing and lift). **Bore and stroke:** 82mm x 85mm; **capacity:** 1796cc; **power:** 189bhp at 7800rpm; **torque:** 133lb/ft at 6800rpm.
GEARBOX: Six-speed.
SUSPENSION: Front: Independent by unequal length double wishbones, single coil-over damper, anti-roll bar; **rear:** Independent by unequal length double wishbones, single coil-over damper.
STEERING: Rack and pinion.
BRAKES: Cast iron cross drilled and ventilated discs all round: 11.1in (28.2cm) diameter; AP twin piston callipers on the front, Brembo single-piston sliding callipers on the rear.
DIMENSIONS: Length: 149.5in (379.7cm); **width:** 68in (172.7cm) (excluding door mirrors); **track:** 57.4in (145.7cm) front, 59.3 (150.7cm) rear; **height:** 45.6in (115.9cm); **wheelbase:** 90.6in (230.1cm).
WEIGHT: 1929lb (875kg).
PERFORMANCE: Top speed: 147mph (237.5kph); **0-62:** 4.9 seconds.

Type 121 Europa S (2006 to 2010)

The Type 121 Europa S was revealed to the public at the 2006 Geneva Motor Show, and went on sale in 2007. Although based on the architecture of the Elise/Exige – a mid-

The Lotus Europa was slightly longer and wider than the Elise. It was intended as a GT car and had a more luxurious interior.

With its all-new styling the Europa was a good looking car, and well suited to its GT role.

engined two-seat coupé with fixed roof – the new Europa used a development of Lotus' small car platform, which was slightly longer and wider. The changes to the chassis and the rest of the car were such that Lotus saw fit to give the car a new Type number: the 121. The new car was envisaged as a two-seat mid-engined GT car with more creature comforts than the Exige and Elise, and, to that end, as well as the small increase in length and width, the car was designed with lower sills and a slightly higher roof to help driver and passenger entry and exit. The car was powered by a GM Ecotec four-cylinder 16-valve DOHC two-litre turbo unit that produced 197bhp, and, combined with the car's low weight of 2194lb (995kg) and a Getrag six-speed gearbox, gave the car a sparkling performance.

The Europa S had the same suspension layout as the Elise, but had 11.3in (28.8cm) front discs. As was fitting for the car's Grand Tourer market, it was fitted out with a nicely trimmed interior that included a built-in satellite navigation unit. The Europa S was followed by the Europa SE for 2008-2009. The SE had wider alloy wheels, and the engine was retuned to offer 222bhp. Suspension spring rates were increased and the dampers modified, resulting in a slightly lower ride height and a lower front end to improve the handling. Larger diameter (12.1in/30.8cm) front discs were fitted, along with new four-piston AP callipers to handle the car's increased performance. Production of the Europa ended in 2010.

Lotus Type 121 Europa specification

ENGINE: GM straight four Z20LER Ecotec, turbocharged DOHC 16-valve. **Europa S:** 197bhp/201lb/ft torque. **Europa SE:** 222bhp/221lb/ft torque.
GEARBOX: Six-speed Getrag F23.
SUSPENSION: Front: Independent by double unequal length wishbones, anti-roll bar. **Rear:** Independent, broad based bottom wishbone, top links, anti-roll bar.
STEERING: Rack and pinion.
BRAKES: Two-piston callipers. Front and rear discs: 11.3in (28.8cm); Europa SE: Four-piston callipers, front disc 12.1in (30.8cm), rear disc 11.3in (28.8cm).
WHEELS AND TYRES: Europa S: Front 175/55 R17, Rear 225/45 R17; **SE:** Front 195/45 ZR 17; rear: 235/40 ZR18.
DIMENSIONS: Length: 153.5in (390cm); **width:** 72.8in (185cm); **height:** 44.1in (112cm); **wheelbase:** 91.7in (233cm).
WEIGHT: 2193.5lb (995kg).
PERFORMANCE: Top speed (Europa): 140mph (225kph); **0-60:** 5.8 seconds; **Top speed (Europa SE):** 146mph (235kph); **0-60:** 5.4 seconds.

The Lotus Type 122 Evora (2006 to 2021)

With the Evora, Lotus moved up a class into the junior supercar category. The Evora has a new three-piece aluminium chassis based on the Elise design.

The Evora was announced in August 2006 when the first styling sketches were publicised. Designed as a 2+2 grand tourer, it was originally envisaged to sit in the range below a new Esprit, which never actually appeared. Development of the new car was rapid, and the first home market examples were produced in December 2008. Further development meant the car was then launched on the US market in October 2009. The Evora was a logical development of the Elise, but larger both physically and in engine size. While the Evora's chassis was like the Elise, built up from glued and riveted aluminium extrusions, it comprised three sections – front, main tub and engine cradle – to give a greater degree of flexibility in terms of the manufacture of different versions.

The first model in the Evora range was powered by an extensively modified Toyota V6 motor, managed by Lotus' own ECU. The 3.5-litre unit produced some 376bhp and drove through a six-speed gearbox, with the option of a six-speed automatic version. The car was clothed in glass fibre panels, and good aerodynamics were fundamental in the design, to ensure low drag and that the car was stable at the high speeds it was capable of.

As a GT car the Evora also had to have decent interior space and be comfortable enough to cover long distances at speed. It was designed to fit the then CEO of Lotus, Mike Kimberley, who was over 6ft tall, meaning that the car had enough room up front for the vast majority of people. The rear seats were small, but adequate for children, and made for useful extra luggage space.

The Evora's suspension followed that of the Elise in that it was independent all round. It had double unequal length wishbones, which, unlike those of the Elise, were made from forged aluminium. This made them both light and strong, and while they weighed the

The Evora had a distinctive look, with its roof panel just meeting the B post. There are still hints of Elise in the treatment of the rear end.

Both longer and wider than the Elise, the Evora was powered by a 3.5-litre Toyota V6. The low sleek lines of the mid-engined sports car are typically Lotus.

same as the Elise items they were twice as stiff.

The Evora's chassis with its central tub and bolt-on front and rear was also redesigned, primarily to make the car less sporty and more user friendly than the Elise. The main changes made to the central tub were to help with driver and passenger comfort – primarily, the width of the sills was reduced to aid passenger ingress and exit and to give more elbow room in the cabin. The door apertures were also designed with decent cutaways on the top rear, again to aid getting in and out of the car. The driver aids extended to the steering, where an hydraulically assisted rack and pinion system was employed.

Like most modern Lotus cars the Evora went through a number of refinements and evolutions, with the first major change, appearing in 2010, being the Evora S. This had a supercharged Toyota V6 and produced 345bhp at 7000rpm. The inclusion of an Eaton TVS (twin-vortex swirl) supercharger also increased the torque across the range by 35lb/ft, giving 295lb/ft at 4500rpm. Also in 2010 was a pair of performance-oriented Type 124 models: the Evora Cup GT4, the Evora GTS, and the Enduro. The Evora Cup GT4 had a 4-litre Toyota Cosworth supercharged motor giving 395bhp, and was designed to compete in the production GT classes. The Evora GT4/GTS was aimed at the GT4 class, and was powered by the Evora S 3.5-litre engine, and six were made. The Enduro was based on the Evora GT4 and was the base model from which the GT4/GTE homologated cars were built. Powered by a normally aspirated 4.0-litre version of the Toyota V6, the cars were aimed at ACO endurance racing at the Nürburgring, Spa and Silverstone 24-hour events. Only six such models were produced.

The pure racing Evora GTE for the GTE and GT4 racing class was introduced in 2011, and then, in 2013, the Type 122 Evora Sports Racer was launched. Available in four colours (Arden Red, Carbon Grey, Nightfall Blue and Aspen White) the Sports Racer was fitted out with pretty much every available extra, including a switchable 'sports mode' for the ECU, which gave sharper throttle response, plus a new rear diffuser and cross-drilled discs. Lotus introduced the road-going Evora GTE in September 2011 on the back of the GTE racer. The road car had a supercharged Toyota V6 producing 440bhp and an AMT Racing transmission. Around 115 were produced.

In 2015 the road range gained a facelift, with the Evora 400 replacing the standard Evora and the Evora S. This new model was still supercharged, but the Eaton unit was swapped for a US-made Edelbrook, which was installed with an intercooler. This new version had a healthy 400bhp, and bodywork modifications gave the car a bit more downforce. The sill width was tweaked again to make the sills a bit narrower, and the dashboard and centre console were was updated.

In 2016 the Evora GT410 was launched. Its supercharged Toyota V6 produced an additional 10bhp, and the front and rear body panels were carbon fibre. It had lighter wheels and battery, and the rear seats were replaced with lighter carbon fibre buckets.

The Type 122 Evora GT430 was launched in 2017. Following the example set by the 410, the 430 had 430bhp and all the 410's weight reductions, as well as a larger carbon fibre adjustable rear wing and forged alloy wheels. Only 60 GT430s were built.

The Evora GT430 Sport appeared in 2017 with black carbon panels, a Zagato-style 'double bubble' roof, and a new front panel with larger air ducting. The bodyshell had revised, and sophisticated, aerodynamic design, including a fixed rear wing that increased downforce by some 211lb. These modifications raised the GT430 Sports top speed to around 196mph (315kph). The GT410 Sport then appeared in 2020 as a slightly more user friendly version of the GT430 Sport. The GT410 Sport's body produced less ground force but was lighter, and, while the engine produced only 410bhp, the performance was still blistering, with a 0-60 time of 3.9 seconds in the manual version.

The final iteration of the Evora was the US-only 2020 Type 122 Evora GT. Its Toyota V6 was supercharged and produced 422bhp and 317lb/ft of torque (332lb/ft in the automatic version), and the car used a mixture of the GT430/GT410 body features to fine-tune the aerodynamics. Performance was good, with the manual having a top speed of 188mph (303kph), and 174mph (280kph) for the auto; both variants had the same 0-60 time of 3.8 seconds. The Evora was replaced in 2022 with the Type 131 Emira.

From the rear the Evora is purposeful and neat looking. This is a GT410 model.

Lotus Type 122 Evora specification

ENGINE: Toyota 2GR-FE, 60-degree V6, 3.5-litre normally aspirated or supercharged V6. **Bore and stroke:** 94mm x 83mm; **capacity:** 3456cc; **power:** output depended on tune, started at 280bhp. **Supercharged Evora S:** 345bhp at 7000rpm; **Evora GT430:** 430bhp.

GEARBOX: Six-speed manual Aisin Type EA60 with limited slip differential, optional six-speed Aisin IPS Automatic.

SUSPENSION: Front: Independent by forged aluminium double wishbones, single Eibach coil springs coil and Bilstein damper, anti-roll bar. **Rear:** Independent by forged aluminium double wishbones, single Eibach coil springs coil and Bilstein damper.

STEERING: Hydraulically assisted rack and pinion.

BRAKES: Ventilated discs all round. 13.8in (35cm) diameter, AP Racing four-piston callipers.

WHEELS AND TYRES: Five-spoke alloy wheels, 8Jx19H2 ET55 (front), 9.5Jx20H2 ET69 (rear). **Tyres:** 235/35 ZR 19 (front); 285/30 ZR20 (rear).

DIMENSIONS: Length: 172.6in (438.5cm); **width:** 72.6in (185.5cm) excluding door mirrors; **track:** 61.57in (156.4cm) front; 62in (157.6cm) rear; **height:** 48.8in (124cm); **wheelbase:** 101.4in (257.5cm).

WEIGHT: Manual: 3153lb (1430kg); **Auto:** 3225lb (1463kg).

Performance: Evora top speed: 162mph (260kph); **0-60:** 4.9 seconds; **Evora GT top speed:** 188mph (303kph); **0-60:** 3.8 seconds.

The Lotus Type 131 Emira (2021 to date)

The Emira was announced in 2021 and went on sale in 2022 as a replacement for the Evora, Exige and Elise. The company introduced the Emira as the last Lotus to be powered by an internal combustion engine. The car was a development of the Evora, but was specified as a two-seat sports car rather than the 2+2 configuration of its predecessor. The Emira shared the Evora's 101.4in wheelbase, but, at 74.6in (189.6cm), was some 2in (5cm) wider and had a wider track front and rear than the Evora.

As well as being slightly larger than the Evora, the Emira was also heavier. The new model's chassis was based on the Evora unit: aluminium extrusions bonded together with adhesive and some rivets to form a central tub, with separate front and rear elements bolted on. The suspension also followed the Evora's example, with double wishbones on the front, and an independent double wishbone system at the rear using the forged aluminium wishbones seen on the Evora.

The Emira was available with two power units, the first being the supercharged and charge-cooled 400bhp Toyota 2GR-FE DOHC V6 with four valves per cylinder coupled to a six-speed manual or six-speed automatic gearbox. The alternative engine was the turbocharged 360bhp Mercedes AMG M139 DOHC straight four, again with four valves per cylinder. The Mercedes-AMG engine was coupled to an eight-speed gearbox. The Emira's brakes were disc all round, 14.56in (37cm) diameter in front and 13.8in (35cm) at the rear, all gripped by four-piston callipers. Hydraulic power steering was fitted.

The Emira was a strict two-seater, losing the small rear seats seen on the Evora, and, like the Evora, was clad in composite body panels that gave the car an exotic and attractive appearance.

The latest and last Lotus petrol-engined sports car is the Emira. Here, a 2024 model basks in the sun at Castle Combe.

Much more sculpted than the Evora, the Emira is a fitting end of the line for Lotus petrol-fuelled sports cars. This example was at the Thruxton circuit in Hampshire.

The rear end of the Emira is very different to that of the Evora. Its sculptured lines and new lights give the car a great and distinctive look.

Many new driver aids were included, such as new ABS emergency braking and cruise control, along with lane changing sensors and rear traffic alert. The Emira's performance was as good as the Evora's with a claimed top speed of 180mph (290kph) or 169mph (272kph) for the 3.5-litre automatic, and the same 180mph (290kph) for the four-cylinder car. The 0-60mph time was 4.2 seconds for the V6, and 4.3 seconds for the four.

In 2025 Lotus revamped the Emira range, introducing the Emira Turbo SE, which was powered by the Mercedes four-cylinder engine producing 400bhp and torque of 354lb/ft. This gave the Emira Turbo SE an increased top speed of 180mph (290kph) and a 0-62mph of 4.0 seconds.

The Emira was a logical development of the Evora, and built on the high standard of the Evora with numerous small improvements and incorporated the latest driver aids as required by current legislation. The Evora is a super high performance vehicle, and, with its sophisticated chassis, light weight, state of the art engines and advanced suspension, it's a fitting car to carry the crown as Lotus' last petrol-powered sports car.

Lotus Emira specification

ENGINE: Toyota 2GR-FE supercharged V6, DOHC, 24-valve: **bore and stroke:** 94mm x 83mm; **capacity:** 3456; **power:** 400bhp at 6800rpm; **torque:** 310 lb/ft. Mercedes-AMG M139 turbocharged in-line four-cylinder, DOHC, 16-valve: **bore and stroke:** 82.565mm x 72.746mm; **capacity:** 1991cc; **power:** 360bhp at 6500rpm; **torque:** 317lb/ft at 5500rpm.

GEARBOX: Toyota engine: six-speed manual or six-speed automatic; **Mercedes-AMG engine:** eight-speed, dual clutch.

SUSPENSION: Front: Independent by forged aluminium double wishbones, single Eibach coil springs coil and Bilstein damper, anti-roll bar. **Rear:** Independent by forged aluminium double wishbones, single Eibach coil springs coil and Bilstein damper.

STEERING: Electro hydraulic assisted rack and pinion.

BRAKES: Ventilated discs all round. 14.56in (37cm) diameter (front), 13.8 in (35cm) diameter (rear). AP Racing four-piston callipers.

WHEELS AND TYRES: Alloys 8.5Jx20 (front), 10.5Jx20 (rear). **Tyres:** 245/35 ZR 20 (front), 295/20 ZR20 (rear).

DIMENSIONS: Length: 173.7in (441.3cm); **width:** 74.6in (189.6cm); **track:** Front 64in (162.4cm), Rear 63.4 (161cm); **height:** 48.6in (123.5cm); **wheelbase:** 101.2in (257cm).

WEIGHT: V6: 3902lb (1770kg); **Straight Four:** 3208lb (1455kg).

PERFORMANCE: Top speed: V6: manual 180mph (290kph), Auto 169mph (272kph); **0-62:** 4.2 seconds.

Top speed: Mercedes-AMG 180mph (290kph); **0-60:** 4.3 seconds.

OUTLIERS: POWERED AND/OR BUILT BY LOTUS

Lotus has collaborated with a number of manufacturers over the years to produce extensively modified cars based on mainstream production models. Lotus had design authority over these cars, allocated them Lotus 'Type' numbers, and built them in-house, either Cheshunt or Hethel, so these are Lotus cars. Never mind that they were derived from humdrum everyday saloons or hatchbacks, the Lotus engineering input makes them all Lotus.

With its distinctive green stripe set against the white bodywork, the Lotus Cortina is instantly recognisable. Lotus badges adorn the grille and rear wings to hint at what's under the bonnet.

Lotus Type 28 Cortina (1963 to 1970)

The Lotus Cortina was the first of a series of cars given a major work-over by Lotus.

With the Cortina, Lotus was lucky to have Ford's then director of motorsport, Walter Hayes, instigating a motorsport programme that meant Ford had the will and the budget to go racing. Ford was planning to go production racing in Group 2, and had the perfect base in the modern two-door Cortina saloon. Lotus already had a close relationship with Ford that had resulted in the Ford 1500 Kent engine's bottom end forming the basis of Lotus' Twin Cam engine, and Lotus' growing success in competition made a collaboration between Lotus and Ford an obvious choice.

With room at the new factory at Cheshunt Lotus was able to take on the build of Ford's latest competition car in 1963, rather clumsily named the 'Ford Consul Cortina Developed by Lotus', but known as the Lotus Cortina by the rest of the world.

Part-assembled two-door Cortina bodyshells were transported from Ford's Dagenham plant to Cheshunt where Lotus added the touches that made the Lotus Cortina such a potent competition car. First off was the engine. This was the Lotus Twin Cam unit first introduced in the Elan, and, with its state-of-the-art specification and 105bhp, moved the Cortina's performance up a level or two. The cars were also supplied with the Elan's close ratio version of Ford's four-speed gearbox, fitted with a lightweight casing extension and a new remote gear lever. The clutch, again from the Elan, was a diaphragm spring item. The front suspension retained the standard layout but was modified with lower, shortened struts and forged control

The Lotus Cortina was a road legal car but made its name in racing. Here is a 1963 Mark 1 on the track at Castle Combe.

Ford was a bit lax when it came to updating the bonnet badge in the 1960s. The Consul Cortina was the original model name.

Another 1963 Mark 1 Lotus Cortina on the track in non-standard colours but still sporting the side stripe. Popular and successful back in the day, the Lotus Cortina is a regular fixture in the current historic racing scene.

arms. To help put the power down the first Lotus Cortinas had extensively modified rear suspension.

While the live rear axle was retained, the suspension system was changed. A pair of radius arms and an 'A' frame was used to locate the axle, with the tip of the A fixed to a new light alloy differential casing, and the arms of the A fixed to the body forward of the axle, close to where the original trailing arms were located. Coil springs over tubular dampers replaced the original leaf springs. While this system improved the car's handling it also put excessive strain on the differential housing, which could bend and cause oil leaks or fracture. The leaking oil could then contaminate the rubber bushes used to locate the A frame, leading to excessive wear. The brakes were modified to cater for the increased performance, with a pair of 9.5in (24.1cm) diameter discs with Girling callipers on the front. The rear retained the Cortina drums, and a vacuum operated servo was located in the engine bay.

The 13in steel wheels were wider than standard at 5.5J. The body was stiffened, both along the base of the rear seat and in the boot's spare wheel well, which meant the spare wheel was relocated to the side of the boot. The battery was relocated from the engine bay into the boot in the interests of weight distribution. The interior was fully trimmed but relatively sparsely furnished, with vinyl seats and door cards. The driver had the instruments presented in a neat binnacle, with a speedometer and rev counter along with oil

Pictured at a Lotus festival at Brands Hatch in 2014, this 1963 Mark 1 Lotus Cortina shows the distinctive 'Ban the Bomb' rear lights of the Cortina.

pressure, water temperature and fuel gauges, and a nice thin wooden rimmed steering wheel. A new centre console was fitted to accommodate the repositioned gear lever. The original Cortina steel door skins, boot lid and bonnet were all replaced with light alloy to save weight, although all the structural steel in the monocoque remained. All the Mark 1 Lotus Cortinas were painted white with a green stripe along the side. Small circular Lotus badges adorned the rear wings and the front grille, and quarter bumpers replaced the full width item on the front. The changes resulted in a car weighing a svelte 1652lb (749.3kg) some 84lb (38kg) lighter than the original saloon. 105bhp, allied to the much improved handing, resulted in a car with sparkling performance and success on the race track.

The first version of the Cortina was

This 1965 Lotus Cortina is set up for classic rallying, with period Alan Mann Racing red and gold livery, rather than the standard white with green stripe.

The Lotus Cortina excelled in road racing and rallying.

produced up until early 1964, after which the first collection of changes were introduced. These saw the one-piece propellor shaft replaced by a two-piece item, and the gearbox with a standard unit that used the Cortina GT gear ratios. At around the same time the light alloy body panels reverted to standard steel items, although alloy items could be specified at extra cost. In late 1964 the entire Cortina range, including the Lotus, got a revised bodyshell, with Ford's new 'AeroFlow' system.

This meant the car now had a full-width front grille and air extractor grilles on the C pillar. Then, in mid-1965, the troublesome rear suspension was replaced with the leaf spring/ twin trailing arm system used on the standard saloon. In total 3306 Mark 1 Lotus Cortinas were produced.

The Mark 2 Cortina replaced the Mark 1 in 1966, and the Lotus version of the Mark 2 arrived in 1967.

Based on the two-door Cortina Mark 2 bodyshell, the car had a name change, becoming the 'Ford Cortina Lotus Mark 2', but the big change was that the car was now build entirely at Dagenham. This was for two reasons: Ford was not very happy with the original Lotus build quality, and, with Lotus due to move to Hethel that year, production would be disrupted and the quality issues would likely get worse.

So the Mark 2 was built on the production line alongside the Cortina GT, with only the engine coming from Lotus. The car was available in a range of Ford standard colours, but the trademark side stripe was not even a factory option but could be painted on by the dealer. Production of the Mark 2 Lotus Cortina ended in 1970 after some 4093 examples were produced.

Lotus Cortina specification

ENGINE: Lotus Twin Cam, cast iron block, light alloy cylinder head, four-cylinder in line, chain-driven DOHC. **Bore and stroke:** 82.55 x 72.75mm; **capacity:** 1558cc; **power:** 105bhp at 5500rpm; **torque:** 108lb/ft at 4000rpm. Twin Weber DCOE carburettors.
GEARBOX: Ford four-speed manual, initially close ratio.
SUSPENSION: Front: MacPherson strut and wishbone, anti-roll bar; **rear:** Initially live axle with A frame, coil-over dampers.
STEERING: Burman recirculating ball.
BRAKES: 9.5in (24.1cm) diameter front discs; 9in (22.9cm) diameter rear drums.
WHEELS AND TYRES: Steel disc, four-stud 5.5J with 6.00x13 tyres.

The Mark 2 Lotus Cortina was a lot more restrained than the Mark 1 and had few modifications under the skin. Only the badges and subtly widened wheels mark this one out as a Lotus, making it a bit of a 'Q' car!

Some Mark 2 Lotus Cortina adopted the striped livery seen on the Mark 1. This red and gold example is in the popular Alan Mann Racing livery. Note the subtle 'Twin Cam' badge on the boot.

Under the bonnet of the Lotus Cortina sits a Lotus Twin Cam engine. This DOHC unit is sitting in a Mark 2 Lotus Cortina.

DIMENSIONS: Length: 166in (421.6cm); **width:** 62.5in (158.7cm); **track:** 51.5in (130.8cm) front; 50.5in (128.3cm) rear; **height:** 55in (139.7cm); **WHEELBASE:** 98.5in (250.2cm).
WEIGHT: 1652lb (749.3kg).
PERFORMANCE: Top Speed 107.5mph (173 kph), 0-60 9.2 seconds.

Lotus Type 81 Sunbeam (1978 to 1983)

Introduced in July 1977 the Chrysler Sunbeam was a three-door Super Mini class hatchback. The need to get the car into production as quickly as possible in the company's Linwood plant in Scotland alongside the Hillman Avenger dictated the reuse of as many parts of the existing Avenger saloon as possible, which, in turn, meant the car was based on a shortened Avenger platform.

The result was a neat, front-engined, rear-wheel drive hatchback which, in order to maintain the body strength, had a high rear lip for the boot and used the rear window as the hatch. The resulting car was not as

Very much in the spirit of the Lotus Cortina, the Talbot Sunbeam Lotus was a road-going rally car powered by the Lotus 911 2.2-litre engine.

The Sunbeam Lotus was a rear-wheel drive three-door hatchback. Powered by a 2-litre Lotus engine it was a fast and capable sports hatchback.

The slant four Lotus 911 engine displaced 2172cc and produced a healthy 150bhp, giving the Talbot Sunbeam Lotus sparkling performance.

As standard the Talbot Lotus Sunbeam had a pair of Marchel driving lamps mounted on the front grille, and distinctive alloy wheels.

advanced as most of its rivals, which had switched to front-wheel drive, transverse engines and had properly engineered rear hatches that opened at floor level to give a flat load area. However, this dated, slightly compromised configuration meant that the car could be competitive in the rally world.

Chrysler commissioned Lotus to develop just such a machine, which would be powered by a new 2173cc version of Lotus' DOHC 16-valve engine. The result was the Sunbeam Lotus, and the new car was unveiled at the Geneva Motor Show in April 1979. However, thanks to rebranding at Chrysler when the car was put on sale it had been renamed the Talbot Sunbeam Lotus.

To produce the car, Lotus opened up a new facility at Ludham Airfield, close to the Lotus plant at Hethel. Each car would be built up at Linwood in 1.6GLS specification, fully trimmed but with no engine or gearbox fitted. Each car's shell had strengthened suspension and gearbox mounts; was fitted with stiffer springs, better dampers, and a 10% larger anti-roll bar; had a pair of Marchel spotlights mounted on the front bumper; and, unique to the Lotus, a set of four-spoke alloy wheels. The new car was then shipped to Ludham where Lotus fitted the engine and ZF five-speed gearbox, and the complete car was then shipped to Talbot's Stoke Works in Coventry for final pre-delivery inspections, before going out to the Talbot dealer network.

The car's competition history was pretty good, with numerous club level successes for privateer drivers. In 1980, Henri Toivonen won the 29th Lombard RAC rally, and, in 1981, the overall success of the car won the World Rally Makers' championship for Talbot.

Initially the cars were offered in Embassy Black with silver side stripes only, but later a light-blue colour scheme was offered. In total only 2308 cars were made between 1977 and 1983, with their demise bought about by the poor sales thanks to the fuel crisis of the late 1970s and the advent of more specialised rally cars.

Lotus Sunbeam specification

ENGINE: Lotus 911 all alloy four-cylinder, chain driven DOHC, 24-valve. **Bore and stroke:** 95.2 x 76.2mm; **capacity:** 2172cc;

power: 150bhp at 5400rpm; **torque:** 154lb/ft at 4800rpm. Twin Dellorto twin-choke carburettors.
GEARBOX: ZF five-speed.
SUSPENSION: Front: Independent, struts and anti-roll bar; **rear:** Live axle, four links, telescopic dampers and coil springs.
STEERING: Rack and pinion.
BRAKES: Front: Discs diameter 9.5in (24.1cm); **rear:** Drums diameter 8in (20.3cm)
WHEELS AND TYRES: Alloy 6Jx13 with 185/70HR13 tyres.
DIMENSIONS: Length: 150.7in (382.9cm); **width:** 63.1in (160.3cm); **height:** 55.3in (140.4cm); **wheelbase:** 95in (241.3cm).
WEIGHT: 2116lb (960kg).
PERFORMANCE: Top speed: 124mph (199.5kph), **0-60:** 8.3 seconds.

Lotus Type 104 Carlton

The Lotus Carlton (or Lotus Omega in left-hand drive configuration) appeared in 1990, the result of the collaboration between Lotus and General Motors. Unlike Lotus' first saloon produced for a big manufacturer, the Lotus Cortina, the new big bruiser was not designed for the racetrack; rather it was designed to be the ultimate sports saloon. While GM wanted the car to give a bit of a boost to the somewhat humdrum Opel and Vauxhall range, Lotus' objective was apparently a bit simpler – build the world's fastest saloon car. All the design objectives were met, and the new Lotus Carlton/Omega created its own class of high performance saloon car, sitting a class above the Ford Sierra Sapphire Cosworth with none of the Cosworth's competition pedigree. What it did have was a major sprinkling of Lotus magic to boost the performance, handling and roadholding, turning a mediocre-at-best saloon into a true autobahn stormer. The car was so fast that some elements of the press and politicians called for it to be banned!

Built on a dedicated production line at Hethel, the starting point for Lotus was a top-of-the-range three-litre Omega/Carlton 24-valve. This was a conventional four-door saloon car, with a straight-six engine up front. A complete car was built at the Opel plant at Russelheim in Germany, then shipped to Lotus

With its low stance, wide alloy wheels, tail spoiler and subtle Lotus badges, this Lotus Carlton looks mean and purposeful.

where it was stripped down and rebuilt to Lotus specification.

The Lotus Carlton was a front-engined, rear-wheel drive, four-door saloon, with a straight-six single overhead cam engine with 24 valves. The standard suspension and the brakes were comprehensively uprated and the bodyshell received wider wheelarches and aerodynamic enhancements. The engine

The Lotus Carlton was badged as a Vauxhall in the UK and an Opel in the rest of Europe. The large air dam and bonnet vents are all that show this the Lotus version of the Carlton.

The Lotus Carlton had so much performance that politicians and the Daily Mail called for it to be banned. This close-up shows the front wheel and the subtle Lotus badging on the car's flanks.

started life as a three-litre unit with a bore and stroke of 95 by 69.8mm, and was stroked to 85mm to give a 646cc increase in capacity to 3615cc and designated the C36GET unit.

The most important element of the engine's transformation was the addition of a pair of Garrett AiResearch T25 turbochargers and Behr intercoolers with a boost limit of 0.7 bar; taking engine output to a strong 377bhp at 5200rpm. The engine was extensively modified to take the extra power, with the block receiving extra webbing to stiffen it. The longer stroke crankshaft was an all-new forged unit, the connecting rods were a new design by Lotus, and the new pistons were forged slipper type made by Mahle. The cylinder head itself was broadly the same as the original, but the combustion chambers were machined to reduce the compression ratio from 10.0:1 to 8.2:1.

Stuck on the end of the engine was a new six-speed gearbox made by ZF and shared with the Chevrolet Corvette ZR-1, and the differential was a limited slip unit shared with the Holden Commodore V8.

The Lotus Carlton's front suspension was independent using MacPherson struts, coil springs and an anti-roll bar. Steering was by the original car's worm and roller system, but had the speed sensitive 'Servotronic' power steering system from the Opel Senator added. The rear suspension was a modified version of the Carlton's original mult-link design, so it was independent with semi trailing arms, progressive rate coil springs with telescopic gas dampers and an anti-roll bar. The self levelling system from the Opel Senator Coupé was adopted to control the camber changes inherent in the original suspension design.

The brakes were all-new with 12.9in (32.8cm) diameter discs sourced from Portland Engineering in Dorset, England, on the front, gripped by four-piston AP callipers. At the rear were 11.8in (30cm) diameter discs gripped by two-piston callipers.

Wheels were 8.5J on the front, with 235/45 ZR17 tyres, and 9.5J on the rear, with 265/40 ZR 17 tyres. Goodyear Eagles were fitted as standard.

Bodywork modifications were extensive, and included a new rear spoiler, a body kit running along the sills, new air vents in the bonnet to get rid of excess heat, and wider wheelarches font and rear to accommodate the wider wheels. The nose, front wings and boot lid got green and yellow Lotus logo badges, and all of the 950 cars produced (630 Opel badged and 320 Vauxhall badged) were painted in Imperial Green and had Anthracite Connolly leather interiors.

The outcome of all these modifications was a bit of a civilised monster. The car's performance bettered many so called supercars, with a top speed of over 170mph and a 0-60 time of just 5.4 seconds. Bear in mind that this was in a large, relatively heavy (3641lb/1652kg) fully equipped luxury four-door saloon with full leather interior and production levels of sound deadening and noise, vibration and harshness reduction, along with room for five passengers and you can see what an achievement the car was.

Lotus Carlton specification

ENGINE: GM Lotus straight-six, 24-valve with twin Garrett AiResearch turbochargers. **Power:** 377bhp at 5200rpm; **torque:** 419lb/ft at 4200rpm.

GEARBOX: Six-speed ZF S6-40 manual.

SUSPENSION: Front: Independent by MacPherson Strut, anti-roll bar; **rear:** Independent, multi-link with semi trailing arms, self levelling, anti-roll bar.

STEERING: GM worm and roller type, speed sensitive power assistance.

BRAKES: Discs all round. **Front:** 13.2in (33cm); **rear:** 12in (30cm).

WHEELS AND TYRES: Ronal 17in five-spoke alloy wheels, 8.5J front, 9.5J rear. Goodyear Eagle tyres, 235/45 ZR 17 front, 265/40 ZR 17 rear.
DIMENSIONS: **Length:** 187.5in (476.3cm); **width:** 76in (193cm); track: 57in (144.8cm) front; 58in (147.3cm) rear; **height:** 56.5in (143.5cm); **wheelbase:** 107.5in (273cm).
WEIGHT: 3649lb (1655kg).
PERFORMANCE: **Top speed:** 176mph (283kph), **0-60:** 5.1 seconds.

Vauxhall VX220

The Vauxhall VX220 (also known as the Opel Speedster in Europe) was a sparse two-seat open sports car designed and built by Lotus at Hethel, and was effectively a variant of the Elise Series 2 although the two cars had very few common parts. The new car had a 3cm longer wheelbase than the Elise S2, and the door sill members were reduced in height to make the car easier to enter and exit. The engine was the 2.2-litre Ecotec four-cylinder unit also used in the Vauxhall/Opel Astra and this was linked to a five-speed Getrag gearbox.

With its aluminium chassis and glass fibre bodyshell, the VX220 was light and agile very much like the Elise and the 145bhp produced by the GM motor gave the VX220 a better performance than the Rover K Series-engined Elise S2. The VX220 was followed by the VX220 Turbo: a 200bhp turbocharged 2.0-litre engined version introduced in 2004.

A limited edition of 50 track-oriented versions of the car, the VXR220 was introduced in 2004. This had larger brakes and lowered suspension to cope with the extra power from the tuned engine, which produced 220bhp. The VX220 was produced for just five years between July 2000 and July 2005.

Vauxhall VX220/Opel Speedster specification

ENGINE: GM straight-four, DOHC 16-valve. Either 2.0-litre Z20LET Turbo 200bhp or 2.2 Litre Ecotec Z22SE; **power:** 145bhp.
GEARBOX: Five-speed Getrag F23.
SUSPENSION: **Front:** Independent by double unequal length wishbones, anti-roll bar; **rear:** Independent, broad based bottom wishbone, top links, anti-roll bar.

The VX220 was built by Lotus alongside the Series 2 Elise. It was powered by Vauxhall's Ecotec 2.2-litre four-cylinder DOHC engine.

STEERING: Rack and pinion.
BRAKES: Discs all round. Front and rear: Ventilated 11.34in (28.8cm) diameter.
WHEELS AND TYRES: Five-spoke alloys, 51/2Jx17 front, 7.5Jx17 rear. **Tyres:** 175/55 front, 225/45 rear.
DIMENSIONS: **Length:** 149.2in (379cm); **width:** 67.2in (170.8cm); **track:** Front: 57.1in (145cm); track Rear: 58.8in (149.4cm); **height:** 43.8in (111.3cm); **wheelbase:** 91.7in (232.9cm).
WEIGHT: Standard 1918lb (870kg), Turbo 2050lb (930kg).
PERFORMANCE: **VX220 top speed:** 134mph (215kph), **0-62:** 5.6 seconds; **Turbo top speed:** 150mph (242kph); **0-62:** 4.7 seconds.

The VX220 was used by Vauxhall as a halo model to promote a sporting image for the brand. It was a very capable and underrated car.

INDEX